The Analyzed Bible

The Analyzed Bible

Genesis

G. Campbell Morgan

BAKER BOOK HOUSE
Grand Rapids, Michigan 49506

First published 1911 by
Fleming H. Revell Company

Paperback edition issued 1983 by
Baker Book House

ISBN: 0-8010-6148-2

PHOTOLITHOPRINTED BY CUSHING - MALLOY, INC.
ANN ARBOR, MICHIGAN, UNITED STATES OF AMERICA

CONTENTS

GENERATION

DEGENERATION

Contents

REGENERATION

Contents

Contents

PREFACE

THE book of Genesis is the book of origins. It deals with the beginnings of the facts and forces in the midst of which humanity lives, in so far as it is necessary for man to know them in order to set his life in right relationship to them. There is nothing final in this book. Things created are not seen in perfection, but rather as prepared for development. Evil is revealed neither as to its first origin nor ultimate development, but only in the beginnings of its operation in human life. The Divine plan of redemption is not fully unfolded, but the first movements in history toward its outworking are clearly revealed.

The main divisions of the book are marked by the phrases " In the beginning God " (i. 1), " Now the serpent " (iii. 1), " Now Jehovah " (xii. 1). The first division

11

tells the story of the beginnings of the material universe. The second division gives an account of how evil entered human history, and traces its first movements. The third division gives the history of the calling of a man, the making of a nation, the creation of a testimony, and thus the preparation for the ultimate coming of a Saviour. These in broad outline are the divisions of the book. The beginnings of created things: Generation, and, at the back of all, God. The beginnings of evil: Degeneration, and, at the back of all, the serpent. The beginnings of the process of restoration: Regeneration, and, at the back of all, Jehovah.

Genesis

GENESIS

" The secret things belong unto the Lord our God: but the things that are revealed belong unto us and to our children for ever, that we may do all the words of this law." In the book of Genesis the " secret things " are taken for granted, and the story is told of the origin of the things that are revealed.

" What is seen hath not been made out of things which do appear." In this writing " what is seen . . . things which do appear " are set in relation to Him Who is not seen, and to the forces which do not appear, in such a way as to show that the seen and apparent are the evidences of the unseen and the hidden.

Our broad scheme of analysis reveals the book as dealing with generation, the origins of material things, and the connection of such with the spiritual in man; degeneration, the introduction of sin into human history, and the consequent degradation of humanity; regeneration, the first Divine movement in human history towards the Saviour, and the consequent hope of human salvation.

A. GENERATION.

The first division is intensive rather than extensive, inclusive rather than exhaustive. In language characterized by great simplicity it treats first of the material order as far as man; and secondly of man, as to his nature and office.

I. OF THE MATERIAL TO MAN

In the first section which treats of the material to man, we have three matters in sequence, demanding our attention; first, an all-inclusive declaration of origin; secondly, a description of a state of ruin, with no account of its cause; and thirdly, the account of the cosmogony of the present order.

i. THE ORIGIN

The origin of material things is declared in the words, " In the beginning God created the heaven and the earth." This declaration stands sublime in its simplicity. It is without date, definition of God, or declaration of process.

The phrase, " in the beginning," leaves the actual age of things material undeclared,

allows for much subsequently to be revealed
and discovered, but claims that however long
the periods occupied in the process, the first
fact is not the material, but God. The word
" Elohim " here translated " God," and
occurring at least five-and-thirty times in this
particular section, suggests the embodiment
of all might, and is written in the plural, according to the Hebrew usage, which employs
the plural as indicative of superlative dignity
and excellence. The word *bara*, here translated " created," is one of three made use of
when referring to the Divine activity in creation ; but it is the one which in the Old Testament is never used save of the activity of God,
and conveys the idea of absolute Power, operating in actual origination.

ii. THE RUIN

Immediately following this simple and sublime statement, a picture is drawn of the earth
in desolation and a waste. There is no logical
connection between the first verse, and the
first part of the second verse. The words of
Isaiah are very emphatic in this connection.
" For thus saith the Lord that created the
heavens ; He is God ; that formed the earth and
made it ; He established it, *He created it not a*

waste, He formed it to be inhabited; I am
the Lord; and there is none else." In another
passage in Isaiah, when foretelling the desolation which will overtake the earth under the
judgment of God, he says, " He shall stretch
over it the line of confusion, and the plummet
of emptiness "; and these words " confusion "
and " emptiness " are the identical words
made use of in Genesis, " waste " and " void."
The first, " waste," or " confusion," conveys
the idea of utter desolation; while the second,
" void," or " emptiness," suggests the most
disastrous failure.

We have no account of the catastrophe
which overtook the earth God had created, but
which He did not create waste; and all speculation is futile.

iii. THE REVEALED COSMOGONY

The first two movements prepare for the
third. The first affirms the fact that the material universe is the creation of God. The
second describes a condition into which this
creation had passed, in order to introduce the
account of the restoration of order, that new
movement of God by which the waste and
desolate earth was restored to fruitfulness and
order as the habitation of man. The account

of the cosmogony falls into two parts, the first
dealing with the activity of restoration; and
the second with the consequent attitude of
rest.

a. RESTORATION

The presentation of the process of restoration reveals first the agents; and secondly the
order.

1. *The Agents*

God is revealed in this restoration in the
threefold fact of His existence.

The first declaration is full of poetic beauty
and suggestiveness, especially if it be read
in the Hebrew form, " And the Spirit of God,
hovering upon the face of the waters "; and
perhaps the thought of the Hebrew word is
best conveyed by the margin of the Revision,
" brooding upon."   Thus the desolate and
waste earth is seen swathed about by the
Spirit of God Who is the Medium of the operation, to fulfilment, of the will of God, as it
is expressed in the words of commandment.

Throughout the whole movement there is
a recurrence of the Hebrew expression, " Then
said God "; and the Word of God is heard,

uttering the sublime commandments which express the will of God, which are immediately realized through the operation of the Spirit of God.

Thus God is seen, uttering the thought of His will in the Word of His mouth; and accomplishing His will through the activity of His Spirit.

2. *The Order*

The will of God, expressed through His Word, and realized by His Spirit, produces an order which is described as proceeding in stages, culminating in man. The first is that of the appearance of light; the second the provision of a firmament, or expanse, separating waters from waters; the third the separation of land from water in the earth, and the appearance of vegetation; the fourth is the appearance of the solar system as sun, moon, and stars take up their appointed places in relation to the earth; the fifth is the production of a new order of life, which we may describe as sentient, in the appearance of fish and fowl; the sixth is that of the coming of an animal life on a higher level than that of fish and fowl; while the final movement is that of the creation of man.

In the consideration of this account there are certain matters which need to be carefully noted. In the first four stages we find nothing other than the bringing of order out of disorder; nothing new is originated. There is simply the manipulation by the Spirit of God of things originally created, in preparation for a new order of being. Through these stages the word describing the activity of God suggests only the manipulation of material already in existence.

When the power of God proceeded to the production of a new order of life, which may be described as sentient, the word *bara* which appears in the first verse of the chapter, is used again. Thus the difference between the sentient life and all that preceded it, is declared to be the result of an act of God, similar to that by which He originated the material universe.

The final movement is that of the creation of man; and so majestic and important a matter is it, that it is described as the result of some special counsel as within the mystery of Deity, " Let Us make man." Here again, while the word used with regard to the first stages is employed in this reference to counsel, when the actual work is referred to, the word *bara* is employed, showing that man again is the result of an entirely new originating activity on the part of God.

Thus the crowning glory of this creation restoration is man, who is presented to us in the image and likeness of God, although the full process is not revealed, nor the deepest truth concerning man's nature declared in this first account. Taking the story as it stands, man is seen as the consummating glory of the material universe, emotional, intellectual, and volitional. The fact of his spiritual nature, which is the deepest secret of all these other matters, is not here declared, and so far there is no reference to his moral nature.

It is interesting thus carefully to note the position of the word " create " (*bara*) in this story. It is used of that first activity of God whereby the material came into being. It is used of that activity of God by which life became sentient. It is used of that activity of God whereby man was made distinct from everything below him. The word " made " (*asah*) is used with the greatest latitude, but never to indicate absolute origination as *bara* is. It always pre-supposes the existence of things which are to be manipulated into new forms.

Thus the story of the origin of those things in the midst of which man finds himself to-

day, affirms that they result from the will and
work of Almighty God; and a definite order is
revealed, which proceeds from lower to higher;
and an activity is declared, whereby great
changes are wrought, even in the process of
development, by the direct and new interference of God.

b. REST

With the creation of man the ultimate
meaning of all preceding him was manifest.
The goal was reached. Contemplating the
process and the issue, God rested on the seventh day, and hallowed it. How long the rest
lasted it is impossible to say. Through all
the description the word " day " is undefined
as to length of period. In the statement which
immediately follows the section, it is declared
that God made earth and heaven in a day,
which cannot mean one day of equal length
with those already referred to, notwithstanding the fact that the Hebrew word is exactly
the same; because all these days were included
in this one day.

Into this rest of God, man entered; and
it continued until the tempter came, and sin
entered. When subsequently, a seventh of
time was definitely set apart and hallowed, it

became a reminder of that rest of God and man, which resulted from the perfect realization of Divine purpose by Divine power; and thus it was also a prophecy of rest to be reached along similar lines. Fundamentally the Sabbath for man was a gracious provision of God, whereby after six days of toil in fellowship with Him, he might rest in the same fellowship, and in thankful contemplation of His work.

II. OF MAN, AS TO NATURE AND
   OFFICE

The supreme subject of this section is man. In the first section the origins of all material things have been dealt with, and it has been clearly seen that the ultimate goal was reached in man.

This is true, whatever theory may be held as to process. If in some respects the process was evolutionary, the involved purpose was man. It is not within the scope of our purpose to discuss these processes. We may, however, describe what is known as the evolutionary process by quotation.

> " The evolution theory of the origin of species is that later species have been developed by continuous differentiation of organs, and modifications of parts from species simpler and less differentiated, and that thus all organic existence, even man himself, may be traced back to a simple cell."

Now if this be true, it is well to remember that according to the Biblical statement, evolution means involution, which means God; and that involved in the original cell, was man. Let it also be remembered that according to this same Biblical account, differentiation has been by the act of God, and by such acts as have separated between the nothing and the something, between life non-sentient and the sentient, between animal life merely, and human life; these particular acts being described by the Hebrew word *bara,* to which we have referred.

On the other hand, if emphasis be laid upon the direct activity of God, the goal is still man, and consequently all before him was preparatory for his coming.

In the present section we have a careful account of the method of the creation of man, laying special emphasis upon the essential fact of his nature, and revealing his consequent relation to the Creator and to creation. The section is introduced by a summary of all that preceded the coming of man. The heaven and earth were *created,* which is a reference to ch. i. 1 ; and they were *made,* which is a reference to ch. i. 3-19. This is a picture of the earth waiting for a man; potential, not prolific. The special dealing with man falls into four parts, in which he is seen created, crowned, conditioned, and completed.

i. CREATED

The creation of man is now described in such a way that the fullest truth concerning his nature may be known. Three distinct movements are recorded in the brief but comprehensive account. First, " Jehovah God formed man of the dust "; second, " Jehovah God . . . breathed into his nostrils the breath of life "; finally, " man became a living soul."

When the prophet Isaiah was delivering his messages, on one remarkable occasion, he made use of three words in describing God's right in man, " I have created, I have formed, I have made " (Isa. xliii. 7). The first of these is the Hebrew word *bara*, already more than once referred to. The last is the word *asah*, already once referred to. The central one, " I have formed," is the Hebrew word *yatsar*, which signifies to form or fashion as a potter does the clay.

This first declaration then, refers to that activity of God which was the first process in the making of a man, that namely of His use of material already existing, for the physical basis. " The Lord God formed man of the dust of the ground." The Duke of Argyll has said,

"The three commonest gases—oxygen, hydrogen, and nitrogen—with carbon and sulphur, are the foundation-stones of man's body. In slightly different proportions these elements constitute the primordial combination of matter which is the abode of life. In the finished structure there appear besides, lime, potash, a little iron, sodium, and phosphorus. These are the constituents of the human body."

Now all these are found in the dust of the ground; and thus, by whatever process from lower to higher, God formed man on the physical side; that is, the animal basis, but it is not man in the image and likeness of God. That physical basis never became man until the second of these processes followed, which is described by the words, "Jehovah God . . . breathed into his nostrils the breath of life." This is the declaration of the final Divine act, mysterious and incomprehensible, wherein God did communicate to that which He had formed out of the dust, His own life, so that man became by that final act, a living soul, in the likeness and image of God.

It is perhaps helpful here to translate that central declaration of the final Divine activity thus, " Jehovah God breathed into his breathing places the breath of lives." This suggests not merely breathing through the nostrils, but the envelopment of the whole animal organism with a new quality of Divine life, which created a new being; a combination, strange and mysterious, of dust and Deity. The crisis of the beginning of that being came with the inbreathing of the breath of lives. Thus man essentially is spirit.

ii. CROWNED

Man, thus created, was placed in a garden. This garden was of Divine planting, and in it man was to find his occupation. The nature of that occupation is at once revealed. Man is to serve in subjection to the will of his Creator. He is to reign over all beneath him. The garden was not the ultimate goal. It was the opportunity for the exercise of the functions of the life bestowed. Within it there lay potentially the city. This city, man was intended to build, by the cultivation of the forces of the garden. His occupation therefore was that of dominion in service. He was to exercise dominion over the earth by dressing and keeping the garden. He was to render submission to a Divine intention, and thus cooperate in a Divine purpose by that self-same activity of dressing and keeping the garden.

iii. CONDITIONED

The life of man in its relation to God and Nature was conditioned by a simple and yet perfectly clear command. This command indicated the limits of liberty. There were things which man might do. There were bounds beyond which he might not go. His liberty was conditioned in his loyalty to the law of his God.

Of these fundamental facts the trees of the garden afforded sacramental symbols. Of all, save one, he was permitted to eat. This was permission to live of the fruit of his own toil. One tree was separated. Of this he might not eat. It was to stand in the presence of his life, marking the bounds of his freedom. It was called the tree of the knowledge of good and evil. Speculation as to what it was, is idle, and beside the mark. The matter of importance is that of the principle involved, that this marvellous being, combining in his personality elements of the dust which are in themselves of Divine origin, with the directly implanted life of God, could only fulfil the highest function of his being as his will was submitted to the will of God.

iv. COMPLETED

In this section we see man using his Divinely bestowed powers in the naming of the living creatures. This was the activity of his intelligence. He was yet, however, incomplete. His being demanded a counterpart. In its very nature it could not fulfil itself save by co-operation. The ultimate purpose of creation was not that of a lonely and self-sufficient being, but that of a great society, bound together by common ties, and acting in such co-operation as should give expression to the multiplied mystery of Deity.

The final act of God in the creation of man was that of supplying his helpmeet. Woman was formed, not directly from the dust of the ground, nor directly by a new outgoing of Deity. She was taken from the man, and is therefore of his nature, combining the material and the spiritual, and being of the man the complement and perfection. Thus in the man and the woman, and not in either alone, the image and the likeness of God are seen. "God created man in His own image, in the image of God created He him; male and female created He them." In God are Fatherhood and Motherhood, parenthood and childhood. In these two beings, in their unity as the crowning glory of His creation, God Himself is revealed. Through all the majestic processes of the past, God had moved with unerring wisdom and unchanging intention towards this self-expression of Himself in humanity, the ultimate meaning of which will only be known in the ages to come.

B. DEGENERATION.

As the first division of the book of Genesis answers questions arising in the presence of the created order; the second division replies to questions arising in view of the facts of sin and suffering and sorrow. How long man remained in the realization of his life according to the Divine purpose we have no means of knowing; certainly not more than a century. Seth was born when Adam was one hundred and thirty years of age, and after Abel's death. Abel was not born until after the Fall, and seeing that he had attained to manhood's age at death, it is evident that the period of human innocence and happiness was not more than a century.

In this section we have the account of the beginnings of human degeneration. The story tells of the degeneration of the individual, of the family, of society; gives the account of the Divine interpolation in judgment and mercy; and then tells of the beginning of national life and of its degeneration.

I. OF THE INDIVIDUAL

In approaching this section of the book of Genesis, the old question naturally arises as to whether the story is literal or allegorical, and in order to our study of the book it is necessary that some brief words be written on the subject. To make the story wholly allegorical is to cut away the foundation of Bible history, and to make it necessary to treat everything subsequently as allegorical. Real flesh-and-blood men are not begotten by myths. All that follows in the history of the Bible, both in Old and New Testaments, has to do with a race springing from a man. This is true even of the central Figure of the Bible, so far as His humanity is concerned. If the historicity of man is recognized, the facts of the story must be accepted as true.

On the other hand, to make the story wholly literal is to deny its fullest value. For instance, if the story be absolutely literal, then the final result of evil is the bruising of the heel of a man, and the bruising of the head of a snake. No one supposes this to be the case. It is perfectly patent that in this connection figures of speech are used.

The facts here recorded, as interpreted by the history which follows, are that we have an account of spiritual transactions in material life. The spirit of evil took material form in order to reach the essential spirit of man through his material being. We must therefore consider the material facts, always watching for the spiritual significance.

The account of the degeneration of the individual falls into two parts; in the first of which the serpent and man are the central figures; while in the second everything gathers around the presence and activity of Jehovah.

i. THE SERPENT AND MAN

The section is introduced by the suggestive phrase, " Now the serpent," and the first matter demanding attention is that of the being thus described. The word translated " serpent " (*nachash*) is derived from a root meaning to hiss or to whisper, and undoubtedly refers to a serpent as we understand the word.

It is at once evident, however, that the being thus described was not, at the time of his appearance to Eve, a reptile, for it is compared with " beasts of the field," and not with " creeping things."

Light is thrown upon the story by Paul, when in writing to the Corinthians he said, " I fear, lest by any means, as the serpent beguiled Eve in his craftiness, your minds should be corrupted "; and a little later in the same connection he declared, " Satan fashioneth himself into an angel of light."

Bearing this in mind we turn to the prophecy of Isaiah, and find that in the course of the burden of Philistia he said, " Rejoice not, O Philistia, all of thee, because the rod that smote thee is broken: for out of the serpent's root shall come forth a basilisk, and his fruit shall be a fiery flying serpent." There the word " serpent " in the phrase " the serpent's root " is the word used in Genesis. Out of this comes literally a flying seraph (*saraph m'opheph*). In the story of the visitation in the wilderness the two words are brought into connection, *nachashim saraphim,* that is, literally, serpents seraphs. Once again, in the great vision of Isaiah the same word is used (*saraph*) of the *seraphim.*

A comparison of these passages will help us to understand the Genesis story. Eve was beguiled by the serpent, that is, Satan, who fashioned himself as an angel of light. In order to appeal to her through the material, he took possession of a beast of the field, more subtle, that is, more cautious than any other; and transformed it into the appearance of a fiery seraph, or in the words of Paul, " an angel of light." If this interpretation be accepted, it is at least more easy to understand the willingness of the woman to listen; and this is in harmony with the whole Biblical revelation of Satan and his methods. In the words of our Lord, " he is a liar and the father thereof," and his method is never that of presenting himself in the naked horror of his evil nature, or of choosing methods of approach which suggest that fact.

Thus the spirit of evil taking material form in order to reach the spirit of man through his material being, made his attack upon the central and vital principle of relationship between man and God, that namely of faith. The deepest note in the attack is that of this attempt to reflect on God. An appeal was made to the curiosity of the woman. She was engaged in a conversation which was aimed at undermining her confidence in God.

The deepest note in the fall of man is that of failure of faith, which issued in disobedience, and proceeded necessarily to death.

Faith being lost, fear immediately succeeded. There was no change in God to warrant the hiding of man from Him. The change had taken place in man. The two principles of faith and fear are eternally antagonistic. Either can only flourish at the expense of the other. So long as faith was the master principle of life, there was no room for fear. The goodness of God being called in question, man attempted the government of his own life by acting upon his own choice, and the first sheaf of the harvest of such action was that of the fear that hath torment.

ii. Jehovah

Man may hide from God, but he cannot escape Him, and it is indeed well that he cannot. In this section we have the account of the insistence of God upon the necessity for the maintenance of the authority of His throne, and a revelation of His determination to exercise that authority in holiness and in love. The movement is fourfold; and consists of inquisition, sentence, prophecy, and exclusion.

a. INQUISITION

The first cry of God thrills with the pathos and tenderness of the pain of His heart. "Where art thou?" Man immediately confessed his fear, and thus was brought to the confession of his sin.

The spirit of pride was manifest in the attempt both of the man and of the woman to escape responsibility; he by attempting to place the blame upon the woman, with a veiled reflection upon God, in that he said, " the woman whom Thou gavest"; and she by blaming the serpent.

The infinite justice of God is manifest in this process of inquisition in that He allowed the man and the woman to state their case; and thus traced back the evil to its original source.

b. SENTENCE

In the sentences pronounced there is evidenced the differentiation of strictest justice. The beast of the field which had been made the medium of Satanic purpose, was changed from one form of life to a lower. It thus became, not consciously to itself, but evidently to humanity, an abiding symbol of the degradation of the arch-enemy, who had slandered God.

The sentence upon the woman was that the distinctive and highest exercise of her nature, that of motherhood, should be associated with sorrow and with pain.

The sentence upon the man was that the highest activity of his life, that of toil, should be accompanied by weariness; that he should earn his bread in the sweat of his brow.

c. PROPHECY

Intermingled with these words of sentence, and shining with the light of the Infinite Love, the earliest prophetic word foretelling a Divinely determined deliverance, broke upon human ears. The seed of the woman coming into being through birth pangs and travail would ultimately become the Deliverer, who through suffering would overcome the destroyer. This prophetic word was emphasized by the clothing of the man and woman in coats of skins. For the hiding of the nakedness of which they had become ashamed, garments were given which were provided at the cost of life.

d. EXCLUSION

Behind all the movements of law, the heart of Love was supreme. This was finally manifest in the exclusion of Adam and Eve from the tree of life, in order that they might not perpetuate the condition into which they had come as the result of sin.

II. OF THE FAMILY

The degeneration of the individual is trans-mitted, and this section covering a period, measuring by the ages of the men, of about fifteen hundred years, reveals the failure of family life; dealing first with the first family; and secondly, in broad outline, with the families succeeding.

i. THE FIRST FAMILY

This is a story full of heart-break and dis-appointment. Eve named her firstborn Cain, meaning Acquisition, evidently in the hope that in him there was fulfilment of the promise that the seed of the woman should bruise the head of the serpent. How little she knew of the real nature of her own sin! This firstborn was manifestly an inheritor of a fallen nature, and in all probability from the beginning there were manifestations of that wayward rebel-liousness, which ever tends to break the heart of fatherhood and motherhood; and which at last brings them to an understanding of the pain of God over their own sin. The second son she called Abel, that is Vanity, and thereby revealed the disappointment which had come to her through Cain.

The break-up of the family ideal is at once

apparent. The brothers differed in the deepest things of their lives. Cain brought as an offering the perfect result of his own toil. Abel also brought an offering which was connected with his calling; but in his offering there was the evidence of a consciousness of the need of sacrifice, resulting from a sense of sin.

The Divine discrimination was manifested in the rejection of Cain's offering, and the acceptance of Abel's. The reason for that discrimination is plainly stated by the writer of the letter to the Hebrews. Abel was a man of faith; Cain was not. The one was godly; the other, in the deep things of his life, was godless. It is not correct to say that one man was accepted and the other rejected because of the difference in their offerings. It is true rather that the offerings were respectively accepted and rejected, because of the difference in the men.

The dealing of Jehovah with Cain was that of a great patience, as He reasoned with him concerning the unreasonableness of his wrath, and told him that if he did well, he would be accepted; and secondly,[1] that if he sinned, yet a sin-offering was provided.

---

[1] It is commonly agreed that the Hebrew word here may mean " sin-offering," or " sin "; and the decision as to which

The first death in the human race came by the way of murder. Death itself was the penalty of sin, but it was first executed by the hand of a sinner.

Again Jehovah came in immediate inquisition and judgment; and the murderer, cringing under the righteous stroke of punishment, uttered the complaint which had in it the element of a craven fear. The sentence was tempered with mercy in that the immediate physical death which he feared was postponed.

The action of the man was that of voluntary separation from God. The sentence, " Cain went out from the presence of Jehovah " does not mean that he escaped from the actual presence of God, for this is not possible to man. It rather indicates the fact that he cut himself off from recognition of the Divine government and response to its claims, and went out to live his life in determined independence.

There follows an account of human progress, notwithstanding human godlessness, which is most remarkable. It is indeed the beginning of a history which continues until this hour; marriage, and children, and the building of a city without God. Seven generations are named, culminating in Lamech, who was the

meaning is accepted in this case must depend upon the general understanding of the passage.

father of a most remarkable family. In Jabal, " the father of such as dwell in tents and have cattle," we see the origination of commercial enterprise; in Jubal, " the father of all such as handle the harp and pipe," we have the initiation of the fine arts; in Tubal-cain, who was " the forger of every cutting instrument of brass and iron," the commencement of mechanical skill; whereas in the fact that Naamah, his sister, is mentioned distinctively, we have the suggestion of the first movement towards the enfranchisement of women.[1]

The whole genius of this progress is crystallized in the song of Lamech. In him we see a man repeating the sin of Cain; but now instead of the cringing fear of Cain, we find the attitude of daring independence as in poetic language he defended himself, and boasted of his safety. The song is the supreme expression of the confidence of a man in his own ability to act without God.

A third son was born to Adam and Eve, and was called Seth, the appointed one, for his mother found in him compensation for the loss of Abel. From this son a new line commenced. Through Abel there was no succession. The posterity of Cain was subsequently swept

---

[1] All this is dealt with in a most interesting way in Dr. Dods' volume in the " Expositor's Bible Series."

away in the Flood. Through Seth, therefore,
the seed of the woman was preserved towards
the ultimate victory.

ii. THE FAMILIES

The monotony of the story of the succession
of families is almost wearisome. Nevertheless the chronicle is full of value, first because
it contains a condensed account of fifteen centuries of human history. The ruin of the race
had come through man's belief in the lie of
Satan, " Ye shall not surely die." Quietly and
persistently through the centuries the Divine
sentence was carried out; and as this section
is carefully read, the continued repetition of
the sentence, " and he died," indicates the vindication of God against the lie of evil. God
is always vindicated in the coming and going
of the centuries.

This chapter, with its account of the ages
of these men, is of value as it reveals how early
history was preserved. Adam was yet alive
when Methusaleh was born, and Methusaleh
was yet alive when Noah was born. Thus
only one person forms a link of connection
between Adam and Noah. The story of Creation and the Fall may have been told by
Adam to Methuselah, and by Methuselah to

Noah. Add to this the fact that Noah lived
to be contemporary with Terah, and probably
with Abraham, and it is seen how few links
there are needed to complete the chain of connection between Adam and the writing of the
history.

The chapter finally is supremely valuable
as it gives us the brief but beautiful picture
of one man, Enoch, who through conformity
to the will of God in life and conduct was
translated that he should not see death; and
thus God is seen vindicating, even in the
midst of all the darkness, His power to
triumph, by grace, over the consequences of
evil, when man reposes his trust in Him.

Seven generations from Adam through Seth
bring us to Enoch, who thus in all probability
would be contemporary with Lamech, the
seventh from Adam through Cain. From
Enoch four generations bring us to the sons of
Noah.

Thus the degeneration of the family is revealed, while yet over the whole history the
light of the Divine purpose is falling; and the
hope and assurance of the ultimate victory of
Grace are maintained.

III. OF SOCIETY

With the passing of the centuries the degeneration of the individual and of the family became that of society at large. The story of that degeneration is briefly but graphically set forth in this section, in which we have an account of the mixture of the seeds; of the result of that mixture; and a portrait in outline of the man who was an exception to the abounding corruption.

i. THE MIXTURE OF THE SEEDS

The plain declaration of the text is that there was inter-marriage between the sons of God and the daughters of men, and that this was the cause of a yet deeper corruption than had been known before.

There have been two distinct interpretations of the meaning of this declaration. One affirms that this was a supernatural intermarrying between angels and women. The other teaches that " the sons of God " were those descendants of Seth who dwelt alone, in separation from the descendants of Cain, maintaining the worship and service of the one God; while " the daughters of men " were the descendants of Cain who had followed in the

wake of their father who went out from the
presence of the Lord, and were living without
any recognition of the government of God.
Again we have to say that it is not within the
scope of our purpose to enter into this discussion, but it is necessary immediately to declare that the first of these views we hold as
utterly unwarranted, and outside the realm of
possibility; involving a conception which is
entirely unnatural, and unwarranted by any
teaching concerning angels or men to be found
within the Divine Library. As in the
genealogy of the Lord Himself in the Gospel
according to Luke, Adam is finally spoken of
as " the son of God "; so we hold that those
who, in association with Him, retained the
worship of God, and yielded allegiance to
Him, are referred to by the term, " the sons
of God."

After a period then, the seed of Cain and
that of Seth came into contact. On the part
of the sons of God there was a lowering of
the standard of loyalty to Him, as they inter-
married with the daughters of the race that
had turned its back upon Him.

In view of this, the Divine determination
of judgment was declared in the words, " My
Spirit shall not strive with man for ever ";
but a definite period of respite was also deter-

mined, that namely of one hundred and twenty years.

The result from the inter-mixture between the two seeds was twofold in the race produced. There was in the first place a definite strengthening of that which was purely physical and of the earth. A race of Nephilim, or giants resulted. The chronicler draws attention to the fact that subsequently, or in his own words, " also after that," a similar result followed a similar activity, " when the sons of God came in unto the daughters of men, and they bare children to them." The only other occasion where Nephilim are referred to is in the Book of Numbers, where they are described as " the sons of Anak " (xiii. 33). As the Nephilim referred to in our section were certainly all swept away by the Flood, those described in Numbers must have been a separate race, springing from a similar cause; but here it is distinctly affirmed that they were the sons of Anak. Anak was the son of Arba, the founder of the city of Kiriath, according to the book of Joshua (xv. 13) ; and Arba is distinctly affirmed to be a man in the same book (xiv. 15). This man is referred to in Genesis twice as the founder of the city which was subsequently named Hebron (xxiii. 2, xxxv. 27). In both cases therefore this kind

of inter-mixture resulted in the production of
a strong physical race.

ii. The Result of the Mixture

The principal result was that of the terrible corruption now graphically described.
The outward manifestation is recorded in the
declaration that " the wickedness of man was
great in the earth." This outward manifestation is accounted for by the fact of an inward
corruption, the terribleness of which is revealed in the statement that " every imagination of the thoughts of his heart was only evil
continually." The imagination, or purpose,
or desire, was absolutely evil; as the significant words, " every," " only," " continually,"
reveal. There was no admixture of good.
There was neither relenting nor repenting.
The picture is one of utter and hopeless de-
pravity. God was forgotten, or defied; and
the flesh, with its passions and lusts, was reg-
nant.

The story of the Divine intervention then
follows. The action of judgment was the result of the intimate knowledge of Jehovah. In
view of the widespread and appalling corruption " it repented the Lord that He had made
man on the earth "; that is to say, His pur-

pose concerning those upon whom He looked was changed, because of their departure from His original purpose for them.

In this connection it should be carefully noticed that beyond this perfect knowledge of the condition, and this change of purpose, there was that deeper fact chronicled in words which startle us as we read, " It grieved Him at His heart." It is important that in reading this passage we should understand that the word " it " in both cases, refers to the corruption of men, " it repented Him," and " it grieved Him." Thus the sin of man is seen causing sorrow to the heart of God; and like a flash of light upon the darkness, the love and grace of His heart shine forth.

Nevertheless, in order to an ultimate salvation, it was absolutely necessary that there should be an immediate judgment. Already the Divine determination has been considered, that the Spirit of God should not always strive with man, but that a respite of one hundred and twenty years should be granted him. The declaration was now definitely made that man must be destroyed " from the face of the ground," because of his corruption.

iii. THE EXCEPTION

Among the prevalent corruption there was at least one man loyal to God; and that man became the instrument through whom it was possible for Jehovah to move forward towards the fulfilment of the deepest purpose of His heart.

Noah was a man who found favour in the eyes of Jehovah. His character is described in the declaration that he " was a righteous man, and blameless in his generations "; and the whole of his conduct is expressed in the statement that he " walked with God."

To this man three sons were born, who shared with him in the immediate work of such co-operation with God by faith, as constituted the method of God for the carrying out of this purpose.

THE DIVINE INTERPOLATION

The story of degeneration is interrupted by the account of the intervention of God in judgment and in mercy, whereby He gave the fallen race a new opportunity. This parenthesis describing this Divine action falls into three parts; the first being a brief restatement of the fact of the corruption of the earth; the second describing the action itself; and the third telling of the new departure issuing therefrom.

i. THE CORRUPTION OF THE EARTH

The fact of the widespread corruption is described in brief but pregnant sentences, "the' earth was corrupt . . . and . . . filled with violence"; and the reason for this corruption was that "all flesh," that is humanity, "had corrupted his way upon the earth." Here the relation between the condition of man and the condition of all creation beneath him is recognized. A fallen man means a ruined earth. At the centre of this description of corruption the declaration is made of the Divine knowledge, "God saw."

ii. The Divine Action

The story of the Divine action is that of preparation; of destruction; and of deliverance.

a. THE PREPARATION

With Noah, the man walking in communion with Him, God held communion, telling him of the impending judgment, and of its reason. Moreover He brought this man into co-operation with Himself for the preservation of a seed, and the bearing of a testimony to the godless world.

Minute instructions were given to Noah for the building of an ark in which he and those associated with him were to find refuge in the day of approaching catastrophe. Through the one hundred and twenty years of respite, during which the ark was being built, Noah was a preacher of righteousness.

God entered into a covenant with this man in which He first definitely announced the method of judgment, that He would bring a flood of waters and destroy everything wherein was breath; and secondly, indicated to him the terms of his responsibility, that he should enter into the ark with his immediate family, and with those living creatures chosen for the perpetuation of their kind on the face of the earth.

The closing declaration, "Thus did Noah, according to all that God commanded him, so did he," is a remarkable revelation of his faith. Through all the period of the building of the ark he lived and worked by faith, being assured that in spite of all appearances to the contrary, the Divine determination must be carried out. It was a period of strange experiences. Godless men of great physical strength were, to all outward seeming, flourishing in material things. There can be no doubt that for material gain they co-operated with Noah in the building of an ark which they must have held in supreme disdain. All the while, by every blow struck, and every foot of work completed, space was given to them to repent, for by the construction of the ark Noah was a preacher of righteousness. Nevertheless it would seem as though none profited, and Noah's carpenters were finally destroyed outside the ark which they had helped to construct.

b. THE DESTRUCTION

At last the work was completed, and the man who by faith had completed that which in the eyes of the world must have been the supreme evidence of his folly, entered, leaving behind him all his material possessions.

Then the stroke of judgment fell. The fountains of the great deep were broken up, the windows of heaven were opened, and the rain fell for forty days and forty nights, until the whole earth was covered, and man and beast, bird and reptile, save such as were within the ark, were destroyed.

The question of the righteousness of this swift judgment can only be raised by such as fail to notice carefully the corruption of the race in its nature and extent. The only way in which it was possible to ensure the eventual purity of the race was by the destruction of that which was utterly and irrevocably impure. Love, illumined by light, acts not merely in the interests of the present moment, but of all the coming centuries. There is a severity which is of the very essence of tenderness; and the story of the Flood is an instance of the activity of the love of God.

Questions as to the universality of the Flood are not relevant to the story as it is written in the book of Genesis. All that this story suggests is that the destruction was co-extensive with the region occupied by man. The Hebrew word used uniformly for the earth

through this section (*erets*), is sometimes
used of the whole earth, sometimes of a part
of it, in the same way in which we may make
use of the word " land." All that this account demands is that we should understand
that a corrupt race was swept away, and a
godly remnant spared.

c. THE DELIVERANCE

Upborne upon the billows of judgment, the
ark of salvation rode securely, holding within
it all that was necessary for a new departure.

At last the work of judgment being fully
accomplished, the waters abated; and the
voice that had commanded Noah to enter,
called him forth. What a stupendous moment
it was in the history of the earth and of the
race when this man emerged from the ark,
which had been in the eyes of the world the evidence of his folly, but which in the economy
of God had proved to be the way of his deliverance, and the vindication of his faith!

He who by faith had renounced everything
in obedience to God, in spite of all appearances, now stepped forth, the sole possessor of
the earth.

By his co-operation with God, a new day
had dawned for the race, in which men would

live, with the testimony of judgment accomplished and deliverance wrought witnessing to them of the issues of sin, and the values of righteousness, within that government of God from which no human being can finally escape.

iii. THE NEW DEPARTURE. NATIONAL.

The final movement in this story of the
Divine activity of judgment gives the account
of the new departure issuing therefrom; dealing in sequence with man in relation to God;
man in relation to creation; the covenant and
its seal; and the beginnings of national life.

a. MAN IN RELATION TO GOD

This brief paragraph is full of significance
as it reveals the first things in the life of Noah,
when coming forth from the ark, he found himself delivered from judgment, and established
in possession. His first look was Godward,
and his first act the erection of an altar, and
the offering of sacrifice.

This attitude and this activity were answered by God in a declaration full of grace.
The sacrifice was acceptable to Him as a manifestation of Noah's sense of the true way of
approach, and the necessary foundation of fellowship. Jehovah's knowledge of the corrupt
nature of humanity is declared, but henceforth He will not deal with sin by judgment
through Nature; and the great promise was
made that the natural order should continue,
the seasons follow each other in regular pro-
cession, and day and night not cease.

b. MAN IN RELATION TO CREATION

The new order was initiated by the bestowment of a blessing upon Noah and his sons,
which was accompanied by the indication of a
new duty, that of replenishing the earth.

The first note of change is found in the word
which declared man's new relation to the lower
orders. In Eden he had governed by love, and
his own inherent kingliness. Through the loss
of that kingliness resulting from the Fall, he
had lost his true power of dominion; and now
that dominion must be exercised by a fear and
dread of him, directly implanted by God in all
the lower orders over which man must rule.

In this connection also an important change
was made in the Divine permission for human
sustenance. In addition to the green herb of
the past, animal food was permitted, while
important restrictions were made in that permission, preparing the way for the whole sac-
rificial system to be made known in process
of time.

An addition, moreover, was made to the law
of human inter-relationship. Henceforth man
was himself to hold in his hand a sword of
justice. A sterner rule than that of family
discipline was set up. Life was safeguarded
by the severe enactment that if it were taken,

whether by beast or man, the one guilty of the offence should pay the penalty by the forfeiture of life. Man, from this time forward, was himself to insist upon obedience to these laws.

This brief statement of the new conditions ended as it began, with the injunction to be fruitful and multiply. The earth was to be re-peopled by a race living under these new conditions.

c. THE COVENANT AND ITS SEAL

In ratification of the promises made in the new order initiated, an actual covenant was now made between God and man, and a token of the covenant chosen and established.

The word "covenant" suggests reciprocal responsibilities. It reminds man that the promises of God are conditional, and that the obedience of man is in that respect conditional also. God will be free not to fulfil His promises if man fails in faithfulness to the terms of His covenant. Man will be free to act independently of God only when he can prove that God has failed in the fulfilment of His word. This covenant was strictly one between God and man, but the whole creation was involved.

This covenant was not now made for the first time, for it was referred to when Noah was taken into the counsel of God concerning coming judgment. It had long existed, though it had never been expressed in exactly these terms. The relation between man and God from the beginning had been that of mutual obligation. Now, however, an addition was made in the promise of God to the race as such, that He would never again destroy by a flood of waters.

A sign of the covenant was chosen and established as such; that namely of the bow in the cloud. We do not for a moment imagine that the rainbow had never appeared until now. All that is necessary is a recognition that at this time God appropriated an existing wonder as the sign and seal of the new terms of the covenant. It was in itself a beautiful and appropriate symbol. The rainbow is the child of sun and rain, and thus is ever significant of judgment in its relation to love.

That bow was made a sign at which man looking, should remember the word of God. It was a sign also to God Himself; for in grace, and in order to enable man to understand that grace, He promised that He would look at the bow and remember. Thus in the contemplation of the bow in the cloud there was established a spiritual union between God and man.

d. THE BEGINNINGS OF THE NATIONS

We now come to the larger outlook upon this new departure. First the sons of Noah are again named as the sources from which the one race would flow into different channels, and so constitute the great nations of the earth.

Then follows a story which can only be spoken of as sad and awe-inspiring. We have considered the new beginning, and immediately are plunged with a startling suddenness into the story of a new fall. Noah had stepped out into a most remarkable opportunity. He stood possessor of a world from which corrupt men had been swept away. He had entered into a new covenant with God, the seal of which was the bow in the cloud. Behind him there lay the impressive experiences through which he had passed; and before him the solemn responsibilities of the coming race. In the midst of these circumstances Noah yielded to fleshly appetite, and became drunk.

In the presence of the degradation of their father, the character of the sons was manifested. One, himself degraded in nature, yielded to curiosity and whispering. Two of them, ashamed of the sin of their father, while yet reverencing him, attempted to hide him, and to cover his shame.

The cursing and the blessing which fell from the lips of Noah were not capricious sentences which he passed upon his sons. They constituted rather a clear statement of the tendency of character. The man in the grip of evil, moves toward slavery; while men influenced by purity and love proceed to government and to blessing. From these men the nations were to spring.

This story in parenthesis ends with the account of the death of Noah.

The account of the beginnings of the nations ends with the story of the dispersion of the sons of Noah and their families after the Flood.

The descendants of Japheth moved toward the islands, or the coast-lands. The descendants of Ham moved toward the plains of Shinar, and thence on. The descendants of Shem moved toward the hill country of the east. It is not possible for us to define very clearly geographically, the districts occupied by these different descendants of Noah. It is perfectly clear, however, that their goings forth were under a direct Divine guidance, even though they may not have been conscious of it.

Christian ethnologists still claim that the races to-day may be clearly traced back to these revealed origins. Paul preaching at Athens declared, not only that God " made of one every nation of men for to dwell on all the face of the earth," but also that He did so, " having determined their appointed seasons, and the bounds of their habitation."

IV. OF THE NATIONS

This is the final section of the division dealing with degeneration. The process of degeneration, from the individual, through the
family and society, has been considered.

Following upon the judgment of God by
means of the Flood, the race entered upon a
new period of its history, and under the guidance of God the descendants of the sons of
Noah were sent forth to the different parts of
the world in order to replenish the earth.
Thus a new national movement was initiated.
This final section tells the story of the degeneration of these nations, and it falls into three
parts; the first dealing with the confederacy
of the nations; the second with the confusion
of tongues; and the third with the continuity
of the Divine purpose through one branch of
the race.

i. CONFEDERACY

In our previous study we saw that the dispersion of the sons of Noah was according to
the purpose of God, and the direction of that
dispersion was under His government.

Now we have the account of a movement
against dispersion, which was a definite act of

rebellion against the government of God. There is first the story of how the people of one language and of one speech, journeying in the east, discovered a plain in the land of Shinar, and dwelt there. This settlement was reactionary, an attempt on the part of these men to ensure solidarity and continuity, by their own wit and wisdom.

Settlement in the plain of Shinar was followed by the building of a city, and then the proposition that a tower should also be built.

The underlying purpose of the building of the tower is revealed in the statement of the people, " Let us make us a name, lest we be scattered abroad upon the face of the whole earth." This scattering of the people upon the face of the earth in order to its replenishing was the purpose of God; and consequently the action of settlement was that of a rebellion against His government.

It is interesting immediately to notice that this plain of Shinar was the site of Babylon, which according to Biblical history had here its beginning, and which plays so large a part in the whole subsequent story of the conflict between good and evil, in the processes of the centuries and millenniums.

ii. Confusion

This rebellious purpose of man was frustrated by the confusion of tongues. Adopting language suited to human understanding, the writer of the story declares that " Jehovah came down to see the city and the tower," which is a declaration of the fact of the Divine knowledge of the doings of men.

His understanding of their purpose is made perfectly clear, and an account is given of how He stayed the process of their rebellious attempt. Men suddenly found themselves speaking in terms which were perfectly intelligible to themselves, but unintelligible to those to whom they were addressed; and therefore, of course, listening to speech that had no meaning to them, while it evidently had meaning for those who were uttering it. It is not at all difficult to imagine the confusion that would ensue.

This is undoubtedly the account of a direct supernatural intervention, and acceptance of the story necessitates belief in the possibility of such definite intervention by God in the affairs of men. Again it is not within our scope to discuss the possibility of these things; but it is well to remember that any argument which is valid against the story of the confusion of tongues at Babel, is equally valid against the account of the gift of tongues at Pentecost.

iii. CONTINUITY

At this point the sacred history is narrowed. The lines of development through Ham and Japheth are omitted, and the generations of Shem are given. This process of elimination constitutes the selection of that branch of the race from which a man was about to be chosen, out of whose loins a new nation would spring, from which, in the fulness of time, the great Deliverer Himself should come.

With this genealogy the division of the book of Genesis specifically dealing with the origins of degeneration comes to an end. Through all the subsequent history the outworking of the principle of degeneration will be manifest, just as through the history already considered, the line toward regeneration has been clearly marked.

The final point of interest in this section is that in its last part we have the record of the first actual movement toward the adoption of a simple faith in God as the one law of life. Terah, born a little over two hundred years after the Flood, in process of time left Ur of the Chaldees. While it is not positively stated that this was in response to a call from God, nor that it was a movement of faith, yet the fact that the movement was in the direction of the Divine intention, would seem to suggest that it was indeed so.

It is to be noticed in this connection, however, that it is recorded concerning Terah, "And Terah . . . went forth . . . to go into the land of Canaan; and they came unto Haran, and dwelt there." If we may believe that this movement, which is distinctly declared to have been one toward Canaan, was indeed in response to a call from God, and a movement of faith; then it is to be observed that it was a step in the right direction, but it lacked persistence. Terah paused half-way, and dwelt at Haran until he died. The reason for the halt is not declared, and perhaps it is wiser not to speculate here beyond that which is revealed.

The final fact then is that the true man of faith, who is to be the father of the new nation, is seen acting so far under the influence of his father, and bound by the earthly tie, abiding with him in Haran until the hour of his death.

C. REGENERATION.

Beginning with the words, " Now, Jehovah said unto Abram," the last division of the book of Genesis is a history of the Divine movement towards regeneration. That movement is traced in its operation in the case of individuals; of the family; of society; and of a nation.

I. OF INDIVIDUALS

The first section in this division, which is by far the largest, deals with the Divine activity in the case of Abraham, Isaac, and Jacob.

i. ABRAHAM

As the matter of fundamental importance in this book is that of the regeneration of the individual, in preparation for all that is to follow; so within that consideration the supreme subject is the Divine dealing with Abraham, and the account of that dealing occupies the largest part of this section.

This proceeds in orderly sequence in the narration of seven distinct communications of Jehovah with this man; interspersed by the

account of three equally distinct deflections
from faith on his part; with certain paren-
theses which chronicle collateral events which
have a bearing upon the main story.

a. FIRST COMMUNICATION OF JEHOVAH

The movement towards regeneration commenced in the Garden of Eden. It had never
ceased in the purpose and economy of God.
Degeneration had wrought itself out through
individual, family, social, and national life;
and now begins the actual working of God in
human history towards the victorious Seed
promised in the Garden.

The first movement was that of the calling
of a man who should be the father and founder
of the nation from which the victorious Seed
should come. In this paragraph we have the
account of the call of Abram by Jehovah. In
the closing paragraph in our study of the previous division of the book of Genesis we saw
Abram acting under the influence of his father,
bound by the earthly tie, and abiding with
Terah in Haran until the hour of Terah's
death. The call of Jehovah now came to him
as a personal call. He was commanded to
sever the ties of all past associations, and to
go forth, governed wholly by the will of God.

The personal element and the principle of obedience are both clearly marked in the direct nature of the appeal made to Abram, "Get thee out . . . I will show thee . . . I will make of thee . . . I will bless thee."

Not only was the call personal, it was also a clear and distinct revelation of purpose. This man was called to be the father of a nation through which "all the families of the earth" were to be blessed.

The obedience of Abram was immediate. He succeeded where Terah had failed. "They went forth to go into the land of Canaan, and into the land of Canaan they came." The contrast with the action of Terah as recorded in the words, "And Terah . . . went forth . . . to go into the land of Canaan; and they came unto Haran, and dwelt there," is striking. Abram moved toward the land, entered into the land, and passed through the land. His companions on the pilgrimage of faith were his wife Sarai, and his nephew Lot. This action was a venture of faith.

b. SECOND COMMUNICATION OF JEHOVAH

The obedience of Abram to the first call of Jehovah prepared the way for further development. Arrived in the land, He immediately appeared to him again, and declared that the land into which he had come would be given to his seed.

Every appearance was against the possibility of the fulfilment of this promise, for " the Canaanite was then in the land."

Faith immediately rose into a higher activity, and conquered in spite of appearances. Abram pitched his tent in the land, and by that act indicated his claim of possession; immediately following this, by the erection of an altar he indicated his allegiance to Jehovah. Thus the tent and the altar became the true expressions of the life of faith. The tent was pitched in the land which Jehovah had promised. It was, nevertheless, a tent, and could be moved at the Divine command. The altar was erected as a symbol of the necessity for sacrifice in approach to God, and also as an indication of his confidence in the possibility of fellowship as he walked in the path of obedience.

c. FIRST DEFLECTION OF ABRAM

The next story is that of a deflection on the part of Abram from the principle of faith. It falls into three parts; the first being the story of his descent into Egypt; the second that of his return to Bethel; and the third that of his separation from Lot.

1. *Down into Egypt*

The cause of the deflection was that of a sore famine in the land. In the presence of this difficulty Abram attempted to make personal arrangements for his own safety by going down into Egypt. Directly a man steps aside from the Divinely marked path, even for reasons which appear to be the most politic, he invariably finds it necessary to take care of himself in other directions than he intended. Approaching Egypt, he was filled with fear on account of Sarai; and he attempted to secure his own safety, and hers, by declaring that she was his sister.

The folly of all such attempts is at once made evident, as we have the startling situation of the chosen mother of the promised Seed in the harem of Pharaoh.

Jehovah, however, guarded the issue of His

own purpose against the mistakes of His instrument, Abram, and by plaguing the house
of Pharaoh, wrought deliverance. The final
picture of Abram in Egypt is full of suggestiveness, as he, the man of faith, the instrument of the Divine purpose, was rebuked by
the pagan king for his dishonesty.

2. *Back to Bethel*

Being thus delivered by the action of God,
Abram set his face again toward the line of
the Divine purpose, and returned to Bethel,
" where his tent had been at the beginning
. . . unto the . . . altar which he had
made there at the first." In this connection
we have a revelation of the victory of faith over
failure. Happy is the man who, having turned
aside from the simple pathway of evident
obedience, in the consciousness of his wrong,
dares to go back to first principles.

3. *The Separation from Lot*

It was at the crisis of this return from Egypt
that separation took place between Abram and
Lot. The occasion was that of strife between
the herdsmen, but the deeper reason was that
of the different principles governing the lives

of the two men. Abram was following God; Lot had been following Abram; and while he also, in his deeper life, desired to be loyal to God, the lack of direct communion with Him resulted in the clouding of his vision, and the lowering of his ideal.

Abram, with that magnanimity and restfulness which ever result from perfect confidence in the guidance of God, counselled separation, and allowed Lot, the younger man, to choose his own location.

In the hour of crisis Lot made his own choice, and it was the choice of a man attempting compromise. The conflict of his desire is revealed in the phrases, " Like the garden of Jehovah . . . like the land of Egypt." If these two things could be made contributory to each other, then he imagined his success would be ensured; and this seemed to be made possible in the plain of the Jordan, where the simple life might yet be cultivated in proximity to the cities which were the centres of commerce. Thus attempting compromise, Lot pitched his tent in the direction of Sodom.

d. THIRD COMMUNICATION OF JEHOVAH

Immediately succeeding the separation between Abram and Lot, and indeed in close connection therewith, we have the account of the third communication of Jehovah, with its record of the word of Jehovah; the response of Abram; and the subsequent and consequent deliverance of Lot.

1. *The Word of Jehovah*

This third communication of Jehovah to Abram is remarkable in that it sets Abram in direct contrast to Lot in every way. Lot, in response to the selfish desire for his own enrichment, had chosen for himself, and now Jehovah declared His choice for Abram. Lot had chosen by sight; he " lifted up his eyes, and beheld." Abram by faith had chosen not to choose for himself, but to leave himself entirely to the direction of Jehovah; and now Jehovah brought him into the place of sight on the basis of his faith. Lot had lifted up his eyes in answer to his own impulse. Now Jehovah commanded Abram, " Lift up now thine eyes," and he did so in answer to the Divine command. Lot having thus chosen, obtained, but was unable to possess. Abram trusting

God, received from Him the title-deeds to all
the land, even including that which Lot had
chosen for himself.

The first word of Jehovah to him was the
command to look, and this was immediately
followed by the twofold promise, first that he
should possess the land; and secondly, that his
seed should be multiplied. The last Divine
word was a command to possess the land, because it was given him by Jehovah.

2. *The Response of Abram*

Abram immediately moved his tent, and
pitched it at Hebron, and there built an altar
to Jehovah.

In this connection his faith is seen moving
on to a yet higher level. It had enabled him
to abandon what were his undoubted rights in
the magnanimity of his treatment of Lot. It
now triumphed again over appearances as it
moved farther into the land which was
possessed not merely by the Canaanite, but
part of which seemed to have become the
possession of Lot.

The strength of faith is most clearly seen
in this action which depended upon the
promise of a seed, which was to be as the dust
of the earth. The fulfilment of such a promise

must at that time have seemed to Abram to be contrary to the probabilities of Nature. Nevertheless he moved farther into the land, to indicate his right therein.

3. *The Deliverance of Lot*

Our next picture reveals Lot and Abram differing in circumstances resulting from the principles upon which they had respectively acted. Lot had chosen upon the basis of compromise. Abram had accepted the choice of God. Lot was in trouble through his association. He had chosen his position, having pitched his tent toward Sodom; and finally, as the narrative reveals, he had moved into Sodom. Desiring Sodom's privileges, he had adopted Sodom's policy, and had become a sharer of Sodom's peril. Abram, the man for whom God had chosen, is seen in the place of separation from the peril, living in quietness and in prosperity.

The Jordan valley was invaded by Chedorlaomer, the king of Elam, in association with three other kings. Against these four, five kings of that region were joined in battle. Chedorlaomer was successful, and carried away spoil from Sodom and Gomorrah, taking Lot with him.

The news of the trouble of Lot was brought
to Abram, and while through his loyalty to
faith he was dwelling in safety in this time
of peril, he was capable of strong sympathy,
and at once went to the help of Lot, gaining a
complete victory over the kings, and bringing
Lot and his whole company back again from
captivity.

The deterioration in the character of Lot
is seen in the fact that while even the king of
Sodom expressed his gratitude to Abram, no
word of thanks is recorded as having been
spoken by Lot. Moreover, so much was his
heart set on the things of Sodom, that notwithstanding this experience, he went back, and
again took up his abode there.

After the conflict with the kings the man
of faith was refreshed by the appearance to
him of Melchizedek. Very remarkable is this
appearance at this point. No other reference
whatever is made to this man Melchizedek,
save by a New Testament writer who uses him
in the matter of his priesthood, as a type of
Christ. The meeting between these two men
was remarkable in every way. Melchizedek
brought out bread and wine, and thus exercised a ministry of sustenance and refreshment
in the case of Abram, who was returning from
a conflict inspired by faith, in which he had

been victorious, but which had undoubtedly
brought weariness, and the need of such help.
On this man of faith Melchizedek pronounced
the blessing of God Most High: and Abram
responded by giving to this king and priest a
tithe of all the spoil.

The king of Sodom in gratitude to Abram
offered him all the goods which he had rescued
from the foe; and Abram refused the reward,
thereby manifesting his faith anew.

The blessing of Melchizedek had been all
that his heart desired, and it is interesting to
note that in refusing the rewards offered by
the king of Sodom, he quoted the very words
of Melchizedek, " God Most High, Possessor
of heaven and earth."

The lessons of this story are obvious. In
the case of Lot it is seen that the voice of
God disobeyed, becomes unheard, and the most
startling circumstances fail to arouse the conscience. In the case of Abram it is seen that
a right attitude toward God creates a right
attitude toward all men. He was eager to
help Lot, recognized the superiority of Melchizedek, and was quick to perceive the danger
of receiving gifts from the King of Sodom.

e. FOURTH COMMUNICATION OF JEHOVAH

The account of the fourth communication of Jehovah with Abram is exceedingly full of beauty, as it sets before us the growing but reverent familiarity of this man of faith with God. In its consideration we shall notice first, the word of Jehovah; secondly, the response of Abram; thirdly, the answer of Jehovah to that response; and finally, the communion between Abram and Jehovah resulting therefrom.

1. *The Word of Jehovah*

That this communication of Jehovah with His servant was directly connected with the events we have been considering, is suggested by the opening words, " after these things "; and the graciousness of its message is even more apparent when this is remembered.

Abram had just passed through two conflicts, the first with kings, the second with the suggestion of enrichment from the treasury of Sodom.

In both he had been victorious, and now the Divine voice declared first, " I am thy shield," which reminded him of the secret of his victory over the kings; and secondly, " I

am . . . thy exceeding great reward," which
reminded him that he had lost nothing
when he refused the reward offered by the king
of Sodom. Jehovah is the shield of men of
faith in the day of conflict, so that they may
rest in Him. Jehovah is the reward of the men
of faith in the hour of temptation, so that they
may wait for Him.

2. *The Response of Abram*

In response to this declaration the faith of
Abram moved on to a still higher level. It
now became strong enough to speak to God of
the temptation to doubt which was in his heart.
Doubts will inevitably be suggested to the men
of faith, and in the economy of God they create
an opportunity for the determined exercise of
faith. Of this opportunity Abram availed himself. The promise of God to him had been
clear and definite, that he should become a
great nation; but he was conscious that hu-
manly speaking, his life was far advanced, and
so far he was childless.

3. *The Answer of Jehovah*

Jehovah answered him with a definite declaration that Eliezer should not be his heir, and

the equally definite promise that a son should be given to him. He then bade him look upon the stars, thus giving him a sign in the heavens, and declaring that his seed should be like those stars. The point of the illustration here is to be found in the words, " If thou be able to tell them." Abram could not do so, but Jehovah could. So was his seed to be. Looking at the stars he knew that there was order where he could not discover it, number where he could not follow it, purpose where he could not trace it; and all that constituted the symbol of the fulfilment of the promise of God to him.

4. *Communion*

Then follows one of the most mystic and yet beautiful pictures of communion between God and man which the book of Genesis contains. The conditions of that communion are revealed in the declaration, which is really at once the conclusion of the former paragraph and the commencement of this. Abram " believed in Jehovah," that is, very literally, he built on Him. Jehovah responded to that faith by counting it to the man for righteousness. Thus Abraham entered into fellowship with Jehovah by faith, and Jehovah entered into fellowship with Abram by grace.

Jehovah now repeated to Abram the promise that he should inherit the land, and Abram asked Him for a sign. This asking for a sign was not the asking of unbelief. Signs are never granted to unbelief. They are granted to faith.

Abram was called to prepare sacrifices, which he immediately did.

There followed a period of waiting, during which Abram in the attitude of worship, drove away the birds that would have settled upon the carcases.

With the going down of the sun he fell into sleep, and a horror of great darkness settled upon him. In that darkness a voice declared to him the future experience of those who would spring from his loins. His seed would leave the land, and go into captivity for four hundred years, and afterwards return with great substance. He, however, would pass in peace to his fathers before these things happened.

This distinct prophecy was followed by a significant vision of a smoking furnace and a lamp; the furnace symbolical of the trial which was to come, and the lamp of the light and leading which would not cease, even in the midst of the days of difficulty.

At the close of the vision Jehovah made a

covenant with His servant, in which He declared that He had given him the land.

It is always a daring thing to seek a sign. If it be done in unbelief, it meets with refusal. If on the contrary it is the request of faith, the answer may bring some revelation full of sadness. The man to whom God can tell His ways must live very near to Him; and even where this fellowship exists, it is a question whether it is not better to walk quietly with Him, than to seek signs from Him.

f. SECOND DEFLECTION OF ABRAM

The previous history of Abram has made it abundantly evident that the principle of faith is the soundest philosophy of life. Faith builds on God, and is satisfied with Him, and thus becomes the source of all righteousness. Faith, therefore, is the highest activity of reason. This truth stands out in startling vividness by contrast with the story of this second deflection of Abram from the pathway of faith. This is the account of the attempt on the part of Abram, at the instigation of Sarai, to realize the purposes of God by human contrivance.

Abram began to reap the harvest of his folly almost immediately in the bitterness that sprang up in his household, and the ultimate flight of Hagar through Sarai's harsh dealing with her.

The far-reaching result of this failure can only be known by a study of the subsequent history. The posterity of Ishmael became a cause of perpetual trouble to the posterity of Isaac. Where faith fails, evil is wrought, the issues of which are far-reaching.

There is a very beautiful part to this story, as it reveals the compassion of the heart of God. Hagar, helpless and undone, fled in her misery to the wilderness; and there the angel

of the Lord appeared to her, and commanding
her to return, promised her that her son should
become a great nation.

Hagar recognized God, and signified that
recognition by naming the well by which she
had in all probability sunk exhausted, Beer-
lahai-roi, that is, The well of the living One
Who seeth me.

g. FIFTH COMMUNICATION OF JEHOVAH

In connection with the fifth communication of Jehovah with Abram we again have the account of a lengthened communion, during which the story alternates between the revelations of Jehovah and the answers of Abram.

1. *The new Unveiling*

This is now the fifth direct communication of Jehovah with Abram, and it opens with a great word, first of affirmation, then of command, and finally of promise.

The affirmation is, " I am God Almighty." This is the first occurrence of this particular title in the book of Genesis, and it is a title which declares, not so much the might of God, as His resources; and the idea of the word would be better conveyed by the title, God All-sufficient, than God Almighty. The root idea of the word here employed would warrant us in saying that the thought is of God as the God of the breasts, the One from whom all supplies for the sustenance of life are gained.

This affirmation prepares the way for the commandment that Abram is to walk before God and be perfect. It is in the strength of the resources of God that man is able thus to walk.

The final word is that of the promise of the covenant between God and His servant.

2. *The Response of Abram*

This word of God gave Abram an enlarged conception of Him. Having known that He was his reward, there now stretched before him a vaster territory than he had known; and in response to this revelation he fell on his face in the attitude of worship, faith rising to a yet higher level as it appropriated the greater revelation.

3. *The Covenant*

The Divine response to this attitude of worship was that of the yet more detailed declaration concerning the covenant; and as in his adoring prostration there had come to him an enlargement of life, that enlargement was signified by the change of his name to such a form that henceforth its very appearance and its every utterance would remind him of the great promise of his God.

In connection with this change of name from Abram, which signified an exalted father, to

Abraham, which signified the father of a multitude, he was promised that the fruit of the covenant should be the making of a great nation, and the coming of kings. Moreover, the covenant was to be continuous in its value, as Jehovah declared that He would establish it between Himself and the seed of Abraham throughout their generations.

Having thus declared the terms of the covenant on the Divine side, Jehovah charged His servant that he also, and his seed throughout their generations, must be true thereto.

This covenant was to be sealed by the symbol of circumcision, which was to be the outward and visible sign of an inward and invisible relationship. It may be observed, in passing, that it is well that we should remember that while this rite was indeed the sign of a spiritual relationship, it was not capricious and cruel, as some have imagined. On the contrary, it was hygienic and beneficent. Medical science in recent years has agreed to the value and wisdom of the rite.

This command was most emphatic and stringent. Not only those born in the house, but those bought with money were made amenable to its requirement.

4. *The Promise of the Son*

Having thus declared the terms of the
covenant, and indicated its sign, Jehovah
changed the name of Abraham's wife from
Sarai, the meaning of which is uncertain, to
Sarah, which signifies a princess, promising
him that she should become the mother of nations.

At this point we find what is perhaps the
key to the whole of this chapter, for in response to this promise, Abraham again fell
upon his face in an attitude of worship, while
in his heart he laughed, and expressed his wonder at the promise made.

There is no evidence that the laughter was
that of unbelief, as it undoubtedly was in the
case of Sarah subsequently. The questions
which he asked are not evidences of failure
of faith. The most natural interpretation of
the story is that his laughter was that of a
great gladness at the bare idea; and even if
the questions which he asked seemed to suggest
doubt, it should be recognized that the fact of
asking them on his face before God, in the attitude of worship, is the supreme evidence of
the triumph of his faith.

5. *The Plea for Ishmael*

In this attitude of adoring joy Abraham gave utterance to something which was evidently occupying his mind.

Ishmael had grown up to be a boy of thirteen years of age, and evidently and naturally had found his way into the heart of the old man. Abraham asked God if Ishmael might be the one through whom the promise was to be fulfilled.

There was nothing in the answer of Jehovah that suggested discipline, but rather a great tenderness, and the re-affirmation of the Divine purpose. God is ever patient with us when the heart clings in affection to some method which is not His own. He never allows the man of faith, however, to have his own way. There is a kindness which would be cruel. There is an apparent cruelty which is of the essence of kindness. God ever adopts the latter as the method of His procedure.

While it was impossible that Ishmael should be the instrument for the fulfilling of the Divine purpose, He nevertheless promised Abraham that he, Ishmael, should become a great nation.

6. *The Obedience of Abraham*

When this period of communication with
Jehovah ended, Abraham acted in immediate
obedience in the circumcision of Ishmael, and
all his household, those born in the house, and
those bought with money.

h. SIXTH COMMUNICATION OF JEHOVAH

In this sixth Divine appearance to Abraham, different phases of relationship between God and Abraham are revealed. Taken as a whole it presents a remarkable picture of fellowship. Jehovah visited Abraham; Abraham provided hospitality for Him; Jehovah reiterated His promise to Abraham; and finally Jehovah and Abraham are seen in co-operation with regard to Sodom.

1. *The Appearance of Jehovah*

Three visitors are spoken of in connection with this manifestation to Abraham, but One is evidently supreme. The three are spoken of as men, while One is subsequently called Jehovah. The two named in the next chapter are called angels.

There can be no reasonable doubt that the third is the Angel-Jehovah Who appears frequently in the history of the Old Testament.

2. *The Hospitality of Abraham*

The picture of Abraham providing for these visitors lovingly and gladly of his best, is a very beautiful one; beautiful in its revelation

of his love and loyalty, but more beautiful still
in its manifestation of the grace of Jehovah,
Who is willing to be the Guest of such as en-
tertain Him.

3. *The reiterated Promise*

We next see Abraham receiving, instead of
giving. Jehovah repeated His gracious promises to him with more of detail, and that
patiently, notwithstanding the laughter of
Sarah, which laughter was tenderly rebuked.

The true life of faith is never taken un-
awares by the goings of God. On the contrary,
it is ever ready and eager to make what provision it can for any manifested need.

4. *Co-operation*

Jehovah now made a communication to His
faithful servant, and the reasons for His doing
so are stated. Abraham in the Divine economy
was the deposit of blessing to all nations. It
was fitting, therefore, that he should know the
meaning of the Divine dealing with Sodom.
Through this declaration made to him, his children would subsequently know that the destruction of Sodom was no mere incident, but
the distinct punishment of unrighteousness.

Abraham was thus provided with an explanation of something about to happen, which would enable him to use it as a warning of vast importance.

The answer of Abraham to the confidence of Jehovah reveals the reason of the intercession which followed. This was based, not so much on his desire to save Sodom or any that were in it, though these matters also had a place in his thought. It was born rather of a consciousness of the strict justice of God, and an anxiety for the vindication of His character among the nations. He declared that God could not destroy the righteous with the wicked, and announced his reason for such declaration in the question, "Shall not the Judge of all the earth do right?" To Abraham such a proceeding would appear to be unrighteous, and he therefore declared that God could not do it.

Upon the basis of this conviction he interceded, and God graciously listened to him, assuring him as his intercession proceeded, that his conviction was right, and that the city would be spared if ten righteous could be found therein.

It is a wonderful picture of the patience of God. He will always listen to honest intercession, even though He knows that His ways are infinitely better than the fears that prompt our prayers. Moreover He answers our spoken requests; and when we have exhausted the limit of our own hope, He goes beyond it, and saves the two or three in whom any trace of the recognition of Himself is to be found, out of the fire.

1. *The Visit of the Angels to Sodom*

This story is a sequel to that of the sixth communication of Jehovah with Abraham. In that, as we have seen, three men appeared, One of Whom was evidently supreme. In this we see two of them who are now described as angels, coming to Lot. The contrast is striking. Lot is seen sitting in the gate of Sodom. By this time he occupied a position of authority, for the phrase is almost equivalent to saying that he had become chief magistrate of the city. This was not the promotion of faith. Success in the eyes of Heaven is of a different kind, and this is revealed in the contrast between the attitude of the angels toward Abraham, and their attitude toward Lot. With the man of faith all three could eat; here the two would hardly enter his dwelling.

Lot knew the sin of his own city, and with great boldness attempted to deliver the men of the city from proposed wickedness, and his visitors from their attempted attack. His defence, however, was quite useless, for the men of Sodom had not been influenced by him toward goodness, and therefore anger was aroused against him.

This story of Lot is full of the most solemn warning. First, he chose selfishly; then he pitched his tent toward Sodom; then he entered in; and finally he occupied a position of chief responsibility. The utter worthlessness of all this success is manifest. The man who attempted to compromise with principle was hated of Sodom, had lost his personal peace; his testimony was paralyzed, and he was utterly unable to influence the city toward righteousness. He was delivered from the threatening of the city by the angels whom he was attempting to defend.

2. *The Plea of Lot with his Sons-in-Law*

His failure is even more strikingly and sadly revealed in the fact that he had not only lost his influence with the city, but with the members of his own family. He had given his children in marriage to the sons of Sodom, and now " he seemed unto his sons-in-law as one that mocked."

3. *The Escape of Lot*

Yet once more the determination in the character of this man is vividly portrayed. In sight of judgment he lingered, and was only

saved as angel hands laid hold on him, and
practically forced him forth. Even when thus
compelled to flee from the coming judgment,
he attempted to make selfish arrangements for
the future, pleading that he might be permitted
to go to Zoar, and his request was granted.
The insidious power of the world is utterly
appalling.

It must be remembered that notwithstanding all this failure, the New Testament describes this man as " just Lot." His deepest
desire was right. His failure was due to his
making an attempt at compromise. Such an
attempt is always disastrous in the life of
faith.

4. *The Divine Judgment*

The destruction of the cities of the plain
was due to an utter corruption following upon
godless prosperity. The stroke of Divine judgment did not fall until the cup of inquity was
full. An opportunity was created for the
manifestation of their guilt in the visit of the
angels. In the attitude of the men of Sodom
toward these visitors, the whole unutterable
pollution flamed forth.

Another evil result of Lot's sojourn in
Sodom is revealed in the fate which overtook
his wife.

The picture of Abraham is very beautiful. He had interceded for Sodom, and now stood in the place where he had met Jehovah, looking toward the cities of the plain. From that position of safety, and yet of pity, he saw the smoke of the burning.

5. *The Secret of Lot's Escape*

As Abraham looked upon the burning cities his prayers were not unanswered, for " God remembered Abraham, and sent Lot out of the midst of the overthrow." Thus the deliverance of Lot was not due to anything in his own life, but to the prevailing intercession of the man of faith.

6. *The Sin of the Daughters of Lot*

The last paragraph in this sad story is a very terrible one, revealing the final effects of the failure of Lot. His daughters, utterly demoralized, were guilty of griveous sin; and in the passing of the centuries, the result of that sin was a perpetual scourge to the men of faith, in the hostility of Moab and Ammon.

i. THIRD DEFLECTION OF ABRAHAM

After his victory over the kings, Abraham journeyed south, and took up his abode in Gerar. This was the centre of a race of men who in all probability had driven out the original possessors of the land, were becoming more and more warlike, and were afterwards to become known as the Philistines.

As Abraham approached, an old fear recurred, and he practised again that dishonesty with regard to Sarah, which had brought him into trouble in Egypt.

Through the medium of a dream, God warned Abimelech of his peril; and in his plea of integrity and innocency addressed to One Whom he recognized as the supreme Lord, there is an evident revelation of the influence produced by the destruction of Sodom and Gomorrah. This is clearly manifest in the form of his question " Lord, wilt Thou slay even a righteous nation? " The answer of God recognized the integrity of the man's heart, and affirmed His care for him, warning him as to what his course of action ought to be.

Again we have the picture of the pagan king, that is, a king outside the covenant of promise and revelation, rebuking this man of faith. The nobility of Abraham is manifest in his open confession of what he had done. The account of the incident closes with the gifts of Abimelech presented to Abraham, and the prayer of Abraham offered for Abimelech.

These deflections from the pathway of a simple and obedient faith in the life of Abraham did not occur in the greater things of his life, but rather in the application of the principle of faith to the smaller details thereof. This was the second time that Abraham attempted in his own wisdom, to steer clear of a danger which he feared; and on each occasion he ran upon the very rocks he dreaded. The results were that the man who stood as a witness for Jehovah, was driven to the practice of deceit, failed in the testimony he ought to have borne, and consequently suffered the degradation of being censured by these men.

Our deflections from faith occur most often through our failure to allow God to undertake in the small matters of life. Some business worry, or home difficulty, or personal danger, drives us to acts that dishonour the Master. That is the man of supreme faith who waits for God in the commonplaces, as well as in the crises.

j. THE FULFILMENT OF PROMISE

At last, in God's set time, and in spite of all natural difficulties, the long-promised son was born, and was named Isaac, which means laughter. When the boy was eight days old, he was circumcized, according to the terms of the covenant between Abraham and Jehovah.

In this connection it is interesting to notice carefully the language of Sarah, " God hath made me to laugh; every one that heareth will laugh with me." She had laughed before, with the laughter of incredulity, and God had rebuked her. Now she laughed again, and declared, " God hath made me to laugh," a striking revelation of the loving tenderness with which God ofttimes turns the incredulous laughter of a fearful heart into the glad laughter of realization. In all the merriment of unbelief there is an admixture of bitterness. There is some laughter that is more sorrowful than any tears. When God causes the heart to laugh, it is always the expression of a full and generous satisfaction. And yet again, laughter God-created is contagious. " Every one that heareth will laugh with me."

k. THE SEPARATION OF ISHMAEL

There is something vivid and startling in
the story which follows. Ishmael, at the time
about sixteen years of age, in all probability
realized that with the birth of Isaac, his hope
of succession had passed away; and it seems
as though he had indulged in merriment at the
expense of Sarah and Isaac; the word translated " mocking " carrying the idea of making
sport.

This attitude of Ishmael was the reason of
Sarah's demand that he and his mother the
Egyptian should be cast out.

The demand filled the heart of Abraham with
grief, because of his love for Ishmael.

In this crisis of difficulty he received the
definite command from God to do as Sarah
demanded, because that in Isaac his seed
would be called. At the same time God
promised that Ishmael should become a nation,
because he also was the seed of Abraham.

Abraham immediately obeyed the Divine
command. Then follows the tender and beautiful story of God's care for Hagar and
Ishmael.

This picture of Hagar's going forth with
her son is full of pathos. It was necessary,
and is of great value in its revelation of the

fact that whatever stands in the way of the purpose of God must be cast out. The principal value of the story is the part the casting out of Ishmael played in the history of Abraham. His presence in the household was a menace, both to its peace, and to Abraham's simple acquiescence in the way of bringing about the Divine end.

In his obedience we see faith triumphing magnificently, for in spite of personal inclination, and in simple obedience to the command of God, he sent the child of the bondwoman forth; and thus leaned back wholly and only upon the Divine provision for the fulfilment of the promise.

PARENTHESIS. THE COVENANT OF ABRAHAM AND ABIMELECH

The account of the covenant which Abraham made with Abimelech is interesting as it reveals an apparent approximation to definite recognition of God on the part of Abimelech. It was certainly based, so far as Abimelech was concerned, upon the clear recognition of the fact that God was with Abraham. In the case of this man, therefore, there was a fulfilment of the Divinely declared purpose of the calling of Abraham, that in him others should be blessed.

It is by no means certain that the word "Abraham" in verse thirty-three is correct. As a matter of fact it is inserted as exposition, not occurring in the actual text; and it is quite as likely, and more so, that Abimelech planted the tree.

This at least seems certain, that notwithstanding the previous failure of Abraham's faith, which had brought about his rebuking by Abimelech, the deeper fact of the existence of his faith in God had influenced this man, and brought him into covenant relationship with God through Abraham.

There seems to be no reason to think that in this covenant made upon the basis of the recognition of God, there was anything contrary to the purpose of God. The friendship existing between these two men as the result of that covenant, based upon that recognition, affords an illustration of the influence which might have been growingly exerted by the people of faith, had they been true to God.

l. SEVENTH COMMUNICATION OF JEHOVAH

The account of the seventh communication of Jehovah with Abraham is one that will always be attractive, not only on account of its own interest, but also because it so constantly finds its counterpart in the experience of the life of faith. In the history of Abraham it was a trial without apparent reason, coming suddenly, and without explanation, and of the most desolating nature. It was, moreover, the hour of a supreme triumph. In the history of Abraham's personal faith it is certain that here we reach the highest height. He passed through the fiercest fires, endured the greatest pressure, as his faith was put to the most tremendous strain, and he triumphed.

The story is told with great simplicity and clearness. We have in orderly succession, the call of God, the response of Abraham, the interference of God, the consequent action of Abraham, and the resulting ratification of the covenant.

1. *The Call of God*

The first declaration is that of the purpose of God in this experience. " God did prove

Abraham." The time of this proving must
be carefully noted. It was "after these
things." Ishmael had been sent out, and the
last hope for the realization of the Divine purpose, apart from the Divinely arranged plan,
was gone. This fact made the test all the more
severe.

The fact that God did prove Abraham is in
itself suggestive. He confers honour when He
proves. He did not prove Lot; Sodom did that.
God proves the man who is proof against
Sodom.

The test was the severest possible. God
asked for Isaac, the one on whom the love of
Abraham was supremely set; but more, the
one through whom, and through whom alone,
the promises of God to Abraham could be fulfilled to all human appearance.

2. *The Response of Abraham*

The obedience of Abraham has often been
described as though it was obedience at the
cost of great suffering. There is no trace in
the Scripture narrative to warrant that view.
That is what we might expect to find, and what
would be found in the case of any man who
was walking by sight. A natural reading of
this story suggests rather that in the case of

Abraham the strength of faith completely overcame all such consciousness of suffering. His obedience was active, ready, and quick; and this because of his absolute faith in God. Rising early in the morning, he made all preparation, and took his journey toward the place appointed.

Arrived there, his word to the young men was a most remarkable revelation of his faith. "Abide ye here with the ass, and I and the lad will go yonder; and we will worship, and come again to you." The verb "come again" is first person plural, as well as the verbs "go" and "worship." We will go . . . we will worship . . . we will come again. The writer of the letter to the Hebrews referring to this, declared he counted that God was able to raise him from the dead; and that is the explanation of this word of faith addressed to the young men. The man who really believes in God is ever able cheerfully to obey Him, because present sacrifice is set in the light of the necessity for the fulfilment of declared purpose. Abraham rested in God rather than in any blessing He bestowed, even though that blessing were Isaac.

The inquiry of Isaac concerning the lamb brought forth an answer from Abraham, which again was a revelation of his faith. "God will provide Himself the lamb for a burnt offering."

The hour for the activity of faith arrived. Abraham's purpose was perfectly manifested in the altar built, his son laid upon it, and his hand uplifted. His intention undoubtedly was to slay his son in obedience to the voice of God, which asked that he should be offered for a burnt offering.

That intention was nerved by the certainty of faith that God was bound by His covenant to raise up seed through that son. To any one acting in obedience to sight only, suffering would have been inevitable, and sacrifice impossible. Faith saw beyond the sacrifice, and was able gladly to obey. We have no right to interpret this story by natural affection which is sense-bound. It must be interpreted by its own simplest statement, and everything in the story testifies to the quick readiness of Abraham's obedience. There is not a single trace of reluctance on the part of Abraham at any point.

3. *The Interference of God*

In the moment when the offering was actually and absolutely made in the will and purpose of the man of faith, the hand of Abra-

ham was arrested by the call of the angel
of Jehovah, and the word of Divine approval.

4. *The Action of Abraham*

The obedience of Abraham was manifested
as conspicuously in the fact that he did not
slay his son, as in his willingness to do so.
Lifting his eyes, he beheld a ram caught in
the thicket, and immediately slew and laid it
upon the altar in the stead of his son. He
named the place Jehovah-jireh, thus testifying
to the fact that the faith that prompted obedience was vindicated in experience. This is the
perpetual experience of those who come to
such an hour of triumphant faith. The only
responsibility is that of obedience. All other,
such as the fulfilment of purpose, is not upon
the man of faith, but upon the God in Whom
his faith reposes.

5. *The Ratification of Covenant*

This obedience on the part of Abraham was
followed by the repetition to him of all the
great and gracious promises made in connection with his calling out from Ur of the Chaldees, and his coming into the land. His faith
was recognized, and the great promises of

blessing were repeated. The blessing resulting from his faith was to fall upon him, upon his seed, and through that seed upon all the nations of the earth. In new strength and new light resulting from this great experience, Abraham returned to Beer-sheba.

Obedience to the call of God, whatever that call may be, is the whole duty of man. The only principle which is equal to the fulfilment of that duty is that of an absolute faith in God. Such faith not only triumphs over suffering, but in the proportion of its strength, cancels it.

PARENTHESIS.   THE SEED OF NAHOR

This is a brief paragraph, the value of which will be discovered later. It gives the account of the posterity of Nahor, the brother of Abraham, as far as Rebekah; and thus prepares the way for the story of the winning of the bride of Isaac, which almost immediately follows.

m. LAST THINGS IN THE LIFE OF ABRAHAM

In this section we have the account of certain matters completing the personal history of Abraham, and preparing the way for that of Isaac. They are those of the death of Sarah; the choosing of a wife for Isaac; and the final records of Abraham.

1. *Death of Sarah*

Here Abraham is seen in the midst of circumstances of natural sorrow which reveal his character. Sarah, who had ever been to him a princess, was taken from his side; and in her removal he lost what undoubtedly had been the strongest human prop to his faith. She had accompanied him all along the pathway of obedience from Ur of the Chaldees. She had shared his darkness and his blessing. She had doubtless sometimes been the cause of fear and of faltering; but more often she had strengthened him.

In this hour of his sorrow, Abraham is seen as a man full of the dignity that results from faith. He was first of all a mourner. These are his first recorded tears. Faith never kills affection, and the man was keenly alive to the

loss he had sustained. Yet sorrow is held in
check by faith; he " rose up from before his
dead."

His action was inspired by faith. He
did not take Sarah back to Ur, but buried her in the land which God had given
him.

His dealing with the sons of Heth concerning the burying-place reveals the true and
necessary independence of one who is dependent upon God. The land was a gift to him
from God, but he would not receive part of
God's gift as a gift from the sons of Heth. He
asked them for a burying-place, and their response was a revelation of the high esteem in
which he was held by the people of the land.
Having obtained their consent, he then
definitely asked for the field containing the
cave of Machpelah. Ephron readily consented,
and then the contract was entered into between them; Abraham offering, and Ephron
accepting, a definite price.

There he buried Sarah, and thus his first
actual possession in the land was a grave. In
this fact there is a teaching and a prophecy.
God ever begins where man ends. The sor-
rows of life reveal a man's true character as
nothing else can. Faith weeps beside its dead,
and then moves out to fulfilment of duty as

it puts a check on sorrow. Faith takes hold on earth's greatest despair, death; and makes it the occasion of a possession which holds within itself all the future.

2. *Choosing a Wife for Isaac*

This chapter is complete in itself, and constitutes a perfect idyll. Its colouring is Eastern and gorgeous, but it is nevertheless full of teaching concerning principles of action. Its place in the history we are considering must not be overlooked, for that history forms a background, giving a true interpretation of the doings of the figures seen in the foreground. There are three clearly defined movements in the story; the commission; the mission; and the marriage.

α. *The Commission*

Abraham was now well stricken in years. Sarah was dead. Isaac, the son of promise, was still unmarried. In the choosing of a bride for his son, Abraham acted upon the one principle of faith. It was of the utmost importance that he should not marry the daughter of a Canaanite. Such a marriage would undoubtedly have meant an alliance which would have given him a human right in the land; but faith declined a disobedient mixture which might have been prompted by policy merely. Neither must Isaac return to Haran. There can be no going back for the seed of faith, even

if the woman sought will not come to him. It
is necessary that a wife should be secured from
his own kindred, and directly under the Divine
guidance, and that she should be willing to
accept the principle of faith, and prove her
acceptance by leaving her own kindred, and
joining the pilgrim of faith in the far country.

In commissioning his servant to seek such
a wife, Abraham asked him to commit himself
to the enterprise by a solemn oath, and after
discussion, Eliezer did so. Abraham had perfect confidence in God in this matter also, as
is evident from his word to Eliezer, " He shall
send His angel before thee, and thou shalt take
a wife for my son from thence."

β. The Mission

The influence of Abraham's faith is seen in
the method adopted by his servant. Having
come " to Mesopotamia, unto the city of
Nahor," he first of all prayed to God. Having
done this he proposed a test, seeking the guidance of God through that test. He asked that
the woman who should be the chosen of God,
should in response to his request for water,
say, " Drink, and I will give thy camels drink
also."

This test was not capricious. It is a clear

revelation of this man Eliezer's appreciation
of character, and his conception of the kind of
wife that would be fitting for his master's son.
Such an answer as he asked for would reveal
a nature characterized by hospitality, simplicity, and humility.

His prayer was answered by the coming of
Rebekah, "very fair to look upon"; simple
and direct of speech, eager and ready to serve.
He immediately marked his recognition of the
Divine guidance by bestowing presents upon
her, and bowing his head in the attitude of
adoring gratitude before God.

This is all very Eastern, and the method of
choosing a bride for another has of course
passed away. Yet surely there are underlying
principles of present and permanent application. Marriage for the people of faith should
ever be entered into within the compass of
the recognition of the Divine government and
guidance. Moreover, the choice of husband or
wife by the children of faith should ever be
based upon character.

Eliezer now entered the home of Bethuel,
being welcomed by Laban, whose words were
those of gracious hospitality, which the narrative leaves us no room to doubt were prompted
largely by the valuable presents which his sister had received. Conscious of the importance

of his mission, Eliezer declined to eat until he
had told his errand. He then laid before the
family the real meaning of his mission; telling
them how Abraham had sent him; how he had
sought the guidance of God; how in the
coming of Rebekah there had been granted to
him the fulfilment of the sign he had asked;
and, finally how, in the presence of that answer, he had bowed his head and worshipped.

As Laban appears before us, his masterful-
ness is at once manifest in the way he acted
as host in the house of his father, and in the
very fact that his name is mentioned before
that of Bethuel, in the consent given for the
departure of Rebekah. Finally Rebekah herself was asked, and her answer, " I will go,"
was surely the answer of faith. In giving it
she was following in the footsteps of Abraham,
as she turned her back upon her country, and
her kindred, to share the fortunes of one whose
very existence was the outcome of faith, and
whose life-principle was also that of faith.
Her going with Eliezer was the going of faith.
However much Rebekah failed in after-life,
there is no reason to doubt that in this story
we see her hearing, not in the same way in
which Abraham did, but nevertheless quite
surely, a call of God, and obeying it in a simplicity full of beauty.

Again the Eastern colouring is picturesque and beautiful as we see the cavalcade passing back over the long distance, carrying Rebekah towards her new home.

γ. *The Marriage*

Isaac, the man of quiet, passive faith, was meditating in the field at eventide, and from that position he saw the advancing company. There Rebekah first saw him, and in answer to her inquiry was informed by Eliezer that this was indeed his master's son. She veiled herself, and approached the meeting. The faithful servant reported to Isaac all the things that he had done; and thus the mission was accomplished in the marriage of Isaac and Rebekah.

Apart from all the details of the far-away land we have a beautiful picture of an ideal marriage. It is that of the union of a man and woman upon the basis of identity of principle. By faith Isaac waited, and by faith Rebekah obeyed. It was, moreover, a union of opposites. In Rebekah, faith was adventurous and bold; in Isaac, it was meditative and meek. Two lives were made one upon the basis of response to a common principle. Two natures, utterly different, yet complementing each other, were

made one in order to the fulfilment of Divine
purpose.

Alas! that in the days to come, through failure, each will be seen degenerating through
response to the purely natural within them,
ungoverned by the principle of faith; degenerating, until Isaac will love a son upon the basis
of receiving venison to feed his fleshly desire;
and Rebekah will stoop to counselling, and arranging deceit for another son, in order to the
accomplishment of that purpose upon which
her faith takes hold.

In the present picture the shadows have not
yet gathered; and the faith of Abraham is seen
rewarded in the union of his son Isaac, a man
of passive faith, with Rebekah, a woman whose
faith was adventurous and bold.

3. *The final Records of Abraham*

The final things concerning Abraham are grouped in this passage, because he is now to pass out of sight; and the history is to gather round Isaac, and proceed to Jacob. We have first the record of the fact that he married another wife, named Keturah; a list of the children born to him of that marriage, and some of their descendants, is given.

Then we have the account of an action by which he separated Isaac from all these, and from all other of his descendants. This he did by the bestowment of all his possessions upon Isaac, with the exception of certain gifts to these descendants. Bestowing gifts upon them, he sent them away from Isaac into the east country, thus leaving him in possession.

The last fact recorded is that of his death, and his burial. This is the account of the passing of one of the most remarkable lives ever lived. It was a life spent in the realm of the supernatural, in the region of vision, and under the constraining sense of the reality and power of the spiritual. Abraham lived not for the flesh, not even for the mind, but for the spirit.

The whole story is told in the suggestive words that he died "an old man and full."

The words " of years " are supplied, and limit
rather than illumine the suggestiveness of the
declaration. As it stands, it is practically a
declaration of the fact that his life was satisfied and rounded out to a beautiful completion.
A very striking testimony to his character is
that of the fact that Isaac and Ishmael united
in the work of laying him to rest in the cave
of Machpelah. They were united by a common
love for their father, whose affection for them
had been very great.

The ending of a life often reveals the deepest
truth concerning its real value. Comparing
the first movements of the faith of Abraham
with his final experiences, creates the conviction that had he seen the end, in all probability
he would never have dared to make the beginning. He started to find a land and to found
a nation, depending wholly upon the promises
of Jehovah. He died with no possession other
than a grave, and with no further sight of his
own posterity than that of his son Isaac, and
his two grandsons, Esau and Jacob, who at
the time of his passing would be about fifteen
years of age.

Yet he died " full," satisfied. The vision
of the pathway is not granted to the men of
faith. It would not be possible for them to
understand it. They need the discipline of life

to prepare them for the developments that await them. Their present duty is very clear. It is that they trust, obey, expect. Where these responsibilities are fulfilled, the end is full of satisfaction, even though to the sight of those who are not acting upon the principle of faith, it may seem to be disappointing, and characterized by failure.

ii. ISAAC

We now come to the section dealing more especially with the life of Isaac; and here we find a man of entirely different type from that of Abraham. In the case of Abraham we have seen faith obedient; and to him the appearances of God were all for purposes of initiation. Isaac was a man in whom faith was passive; and the two Divine appearances chronicled were for purposes of ratification. The story may be divided into three parts, the first being introductory; the second giving the account of the first appearance of Jehovah; and the third, that of His second appearance.

a. INTRODUCTORY

The section opens with the declaration that after the death of Abraham, the blessing of God rested upon Isaac. Coupled with that affirmation is the statement that he dwelt by the well Beer-lahai-roi. This statement in itself is suggestive of the character of the man. He was quiet and meditative, content to abide by the wells, where his flocks might be well watered. He was evidently a man passive rather than active, whose faith was likely to produce quietness rather than initiation.

The generations of Ishmael are now given, together with the account of his death.

In order to give the generations of Isaac, the narrative at this point goes back fifteen years prior to the death of Abraham and records the birth of Esau and Jacob. Before their birth Jehovah made a distinct communication to their mother of the fact that the elder would become the servant of the younger; and this direct word from God must not be forgotten in subsequent considerations of the actions of Isaac, Rebekah, and Jacob.

The two brothers, Esau and Jacob, are placed before us in this paragraph in strong contrast. The first was wild and romantic; the second, as the margin reads, harmless, or perfect, dwelling in the tents. This is a very interesting statement at the beginning of a story in which so much will be seen of Jacob, which is mean and contemptible. Here we have a revelation of his temperament. He was quiet, and desired more the peace of the tent, than the excitement of movement. In the light of this, the long journey and prolonged absence from home will be seen to be the result following his deceit, which was in itself distasteful to him.

Degeneration in the character of Isaac is evidently marked in the statement that his love for Esau was caused by the fact that he ate of his venison.

In the story of the birthright, neither Esau nor Jacob is to be admired. The one was profane, in that he allowed the lower side of his nature to master him; and sold his birthright in order to appease his physical hunger. The other was mean, in that he took advantage of that hunger to obtain the birthright.

b. FIRST APPEARANCE. CONTINUITY OF
   COVENANT

We come next to the account of the first direct communication of Jehovah to Isaac. Its occasion was that of a time of difficulty, such as had caused his father to go down into Egypt. Jehovah warned him against repeating the folly, and the warning note was emphasized by the declaration of the continuity of the covenant, which had been made with his father, and the repetition of the great promises uttered to him.

Strangely enough, though he was thus saved by direct Divine intervention from his father's mistake, and the sin which followed it, he nevertheless repeated the folly of his father in Gerar in connection with Abimelech. It is by no means certain that this Abimelech is the same. It is quite probable that he was the son of the one with whom Abraham made a covenant. As in the case of his father, this man of faith was rebuked by the man outside the covenant, who then charged his people that Isaac was not to be molested.

After this appearance, Isaac gave himself to the culture of the land, and increased greatly in wealth.

The Philistines, with whom Abraham had dwelt, began to manifest a certain measure of hostility, filling up wells which the servants of Abraham had dug. The quiet patience of Isaac is manifested in the matter of these wells. He first proceeded to dig again the wells of his father Abraham. His servants then dug a new well, for which the Philistine herdsmen contended, and he called it Esek, that is, contention. Persevering, they dug another, and there was yet more strife. He named the second Sitnah, thus indicating the increasing difficulty of the situation, for the name means enmity. Once more they dug, and no contention followed.

c. SECOND APPEARANCE.   RATIFICATION OF
    COVENANT

There now occurred a change. Isaac returned from Gerar to Beer-sheba, and Jehovah immediately made the second direct communication to him. It would seem as though this communication was the result of his return to his proper abode. It was of the nature of the ratification of the covenant.

Isaac immediately responded in such way as to indicate his fidelity of heart to the principle of faith. He built an altar, pitched his tent, and dug a well.

This second appearance of Jehovah to Isaac was followed by a visit from Abimelech, who in company with his friend Ahuzzath and Phicol, the captain of his host, sought the establishment of a covenant. To this Isaac responded, by preparing them a feast, and entering into the covenant which they desired.

One brief word reveals the fact that Esau was giving himself up to a wild and reckless life, which was devoid of the principle of faith in God. He married daughters of the land, and caused grief to the hearts of his father and mother.

Isaac was pre-eminently the man of peace, and his principal physical activity, that of the digging of wells, was, as is so often the case, symbolic of his temperament. Notwithstanding his failure, the general impression is that of the faith of the man; and from his story we learn how faith operates in the case of quieter natures. Such men dig wells which are for the blessing of subsequent generations.

iii. JACOB

The history now passes to centre largely around Jacob; and at once we find ourselves in the presence of a man of another temperament, and shall see faith operating no longer in the case of a man obedient, by way of initiation; nor in that of a man passive, in answer to ratification; but rather in that of a man restless, and yielding to correction. The history of Jacob consists of the account of five Divine communications with the man, in each case rendered necessary in order to correction. These five communications may thus be classified; duplicity, and the over-ruling God; success, and the interfering God; independence, and the conquering God; compromise, and the restoring God; obedience, and the rewarding God.

a. FIRST DIVINE COMMUNICATION. DUPLICITY, AND THE OVER-RULING GOD

In this we have the account of the deceit of Rebekah; the flight of Jacob; and the Divine appearing.

1. *The Deceit of Rebekah and Jacob*

In this section four persons stand out before us, Isaac, Rebekah, Esau, and Jacob, and not one of them is admirable.

Isaac was now even more degenerate and seems to have been wholly occupied with his stomach, and anxious for another meal of venison before he died.

Rebekah did not share the sleepiness of her husband. She was keen, alert, acute; and in this connection was revealed at her very worst. She knew the purpose of God for Jacob, but was not content to wait. By the most despicable deceit she attempted to secure the blessing to Jacob. She was aware of Isaac's love for Esau, and against that she plotted. Her wrong was not that of desiring to fix the blessing upon Jacob, for this she knew to be according to Divine intention; it was wholly that of the method which she adopted.

Esau was still the same wild, dashing, impulsive hunter. Jacob was the only one in whom one trait of excellence was manifest. He at least raised a protest, and did not desire to appear to his father as a deceiver; but even here the motive was low, for he was afraid of the personal curse that might follow a discovery; and in any case there was no real excuse for his yielding to the suggestion of his mother, for he was not a child, but a man, bordering on seventy years of age.

The deceit of Jacob, actually practised, creates a pitiful and pathetic picture. He came into the presence of his father with a positive lie upon his lips; to be followed by a blasphemous lie in explanation. He declared that he was Esau; and accounted for the speed with which he had procured the venison, by declaring that Jehovah had helped him. He approached his father silently, lying as he held out his hands to him, and repeating his lie when questioned.

A lie is ever prolific in its propagation. One succeeds another in quick succession, each made necessary by its predecessor. How much more would be gained if men would only learn the ease and simplicity of truth.

Watching the scene, with all the facts in mind—which, of course, were not present to the mind of Isaac—a great sense of the over-ruling of God inevitably possesses the soul. The words of the covenant blessing were generous and gracious as they fell from the lips of Isaac. He imagined that contrary to the declared purpose at the birth of the boys, he was pronouncing these words upon Esau. It was not so, for over-ruling the duplicity and

sin of the actors in the scene, God compelled
the words of blessing to rest upon the man of
His choice. Failure of faith expressing itself
in deceit, must inevitably bring, as the sequel
will show, sorrow upon sorrow. It can not,
however, finally interfere with the accomplishment of the purposes of Jehovah.

The harvest was swift and sure. A lie can
not long maintain the appearance of truth.
Deceit must be known as deceit. With the
coming of Esau there was discovery, and immediate and inevitable results followed.
Isaac trembled exceedingly. It was a strange
trembling, and in all probability had in it
more of the sense of the overruling majesty
of God than of the disappointment of his own
wrong purpose. This would seem to have been
so from the fact that Isaac refused to change
what he had done, or to unsay what he had
said. Therein his faith was manifest. Indeed,
this is the one instance of his faith referred
to by the writer of the letter to the Hebrews.
Through failure of faith he had attempted to
fasten the covenant blessing upon Esau.
When he discovered what had really happened,
in faith he yielded to the clear over-ruling of
God.

From the heart of Esau there came a terrible wail; thrilling with disappointment,

vibrant with passion, and followed by bitter
tears. He was now reaping the harvest of
the selling of his birthright for a mess of pot-
tage. He had long abandoned himself to the
passions of the flesh, even though, as it would
seem, he felt some interest in his father's blessing. In the consciousness that he had lost
that which he coveted, he broke out into a
paroxysm of anger and grief.

2. *The Flight of Jacob*

Still the sheaves of harvest were gathered.
The hatred of Esau for Jacob naturally created anxiety in the mind of Rebekah. She
began at once to arrange to send Jacob out
of the reach of danger. In all probability she
never saw him again, for, although we have
no record of her death and burial, it would
seem likely that she had died before his return.
For Jacob the harvest consisted in this en-
forced absence from his home. As we saw
in a previous study, he was a quiet man, and
a dweller in tents, differing from Esau in this
particular. To him, home meant far more
than to his brother; and this severance therefrom, and this flight to Paddan-aram must
have cost him much. That Rebekah suffered
in all those after-years is evident from the

words with which she sent him away. Her
plan was that he should tarry with Laban a
few days only, and she distinctly declared her
intention to send for him again. This she
never did. We constantly attempt to comfort
our hearts with the idea that we can manipulate the results of sin, so as to make them less
hard to bear; and then we have to prove,
through long and bitter experiences, that this
is not so. There is only one moment in which
we can save ourselves from sin, and that is
before we commit it.

Isaac took farewell of his son, charging him
to seek a wife from Paddan-aram, and pronouncing upon him the words of blessing.

PARENTHESIS. THE ACTION OF ESAU

Esau, observing the action of Jacob, and
hoping to please his father, took a wife of
the daughters of Ishmael.

3. *The Divine Appearing*

We now come to the first of the direct
Divine communications to Jacob. Deceit had
wrought itself out at last, so that Jacob was
in flight from Beer-sheba. Weary with the

journey, he arrived at Luz; and during the sleep of the night he was given a dream.

The vision of the ladder and the angels was suggestive of the possibility and actuality of communication between heaven and earth. Yet that which impressed Jacob does not seem to have been this part of the vision, but the fact that Jehovah appeared to him, and spoke to him.

The message was full of infinite grace. Jehovah declared Himself to be the God of Abraham, and of Isaac, and then repeated to Jacob the promise of the land, and of the seed; adding to this the promise of His own presence with him in his wanderings; and the declaration that he should yet again be brought into the land.

The vision and the voice that came to him in that dream accomplished their end, for on awaking Jacob declared his new consciousness of the presence of God. It is remarkable that he did not speak of that Presence as of a visit, but rather as of an abiding fact. He suggested, moreover, his conviction that God had been there before the vision was granted, for he said, " I knew it not." It is not to be wondered at that such a communication filled him with a sense of awe, compelling him to exclaim, " How dreadful is this place!"

In the morning he acted in such a way as to manifest the two sides of his nature. His deep religious conviction and faith were indicated by his setting up of a stone, his anointing it with oil, and his naming of the place Beth-el, which signifies the house of God. His restless activity and keen managing meanness were manifested in the bargaining spirit in which he expressed himself. Jehovah had promised to be with him, and now he said that if this promise were fulfilled he would give a tenth of all he possessed to God.

It was faith assuredly, but it moved on a low level. Such faith will not bear comparison with that which enables a man to turn his back upon kindred and friends, not knowing where he is going. Nevertheless, it is evident that by this appearance of Jehovah to Jacob he was arrested, and the spirit of his coming to the house of Laban was changed. There were yet many lessons for him to learn; and long years elapsed before, in perfect submission, he worshipped, leaning on his staff. This much, however, was gained. The memory of the midnight vision, and the consequent certainty of the Divine presence abode with him.

b. SECOND DIVINE COMMUNICATION.   SUCCESS,
    AND THE INTERFERING GOD

This section deals with the next period in
the life of Jacob, in which for twenty years
he was a sojourner in the " land of the children of the east," and during which he
amassed his great wealth. It was the period
of his dealings with Laban. On the human
side it is the story of the conflict of two strong,
astute men. There is little to admire in the
methods of either. Of the two, however, as
we shall see, Laban was by far the more to
be despised. The section chronicles the events
of the sojourn with Laban; and briefly records
the Divine communication which put an end
to the period.

1. *The Sojourn with Laban*

The history of these years may be divided
into three parts; that dealing with the arrival;
that telling the story of fourteen years; and
that giving the account of the last six years.

α. Arrival

Arriving in the neighbourhood of Laban's
home Jacob found himself in the midst of pas-

toral conditions, which are described briefly but clearly. He came upon a field in which a well was situated, and three flocks of sheep were reposing, waiting for the hour of watering. The method by which this was done is described. When all the flocks were gathered, the stone was rolled from the mouth of the well, the sheep were watered, and the stone was replaced.

Jacob at once entered into conversation with the shepherds by making inquiry after Laban, in response to which they told him that Laban was known to them, that he was well, and that he would soon be able for himself to see his daughter Rachel, who was in the habit of bringing her father's sheep to the water.

Not knowing their custom of waiting till all the flocks were gathered, and perhaps desirous to have them out of the way before the arrival of Rachel, he urged them to water their flocks and depart. While he was still in conversation with them, Rachel arrived with her sheep. The story of this meeting is the one touch of beauty in the chapter. There is no doubt that it is a pure love story, and all the subsequent history of Jacob shows how dear to his heart was this woman of the pastoral life, the shepherdess of her father's sheep.

The introduction to her was that of his action in rolling away the stone from the mouth of the well, and watering the flock which she brought. This was followed by his greeting, and his making known of his relationship to her. As all the experiences of his leaving home, and the long journey crowded upon him, and as he was conscious of being near to his mother's people, he was overcome by emotion.

Rachel hurried back, and told her father Laban of the fact of the arrival of Jacob; and Laban immediately hastened to meet him, and to welcome him with all the tokens of gladness. After a month's sojourn with them, Laban proposed that Jacob should enter into some definite arrangement with him as to the service he should render.

Laban's two daughters, Leah and Rachel, are introduced to us at this point, and the historian declares that the former was a plain woman, while Rachel was beautiful in form and feature. Laban's proposition was Jacob's opportunity; and he offered to serve Laban for seven years for Rachel. This offer Laban accepted.

β. The Fourteen Years

The story of fourteen years is told as to the actual events with some brevity, while for

purposes of the subsequent history the account
of the children which were born to Jacob during the second half of the period is given in
greater fulness. The account of the first seven
years is dismissed in one brief statement
which is, nevertheless, full of beauty. They
were years in the life of Jacob full of bright-
ness, in which all the arduous work, which he
afterwards described with some bitterness
when chiding with Laban (xxxi. 38-40), was
transfigured by his love for Rachel.

At the end of the story of the first seven
years we have the account of the marriage.
There can be no doubt that Laban, with the
shrewdness which characterized him, had seen
at the beginning how much he would gain
from the services of Jacob, and that therefore
he had readily promised him Rachel to wife.
The true nature of the man is first manifested
in the brutal deceit he practised upon Jacob
at the end of the seven years. Love is, however, stronger than all opposing forces, and
Jacob served again another seven years for
Rachel. It is to be carefully noted that he
married her a week after his marriage with
Leah; and thus the second seven years were
years in which Jacob lived with Leah and
Rachel, as his wives.

As we read the story of the birth of the chil-

dren of Jacob we must not forget that we are
looking at things in a far-distant time, and,
therefore, must make all necessary allowances
for the imperfect light in which these people
lived. Such allowance, however, will not prevent our seeing how much that is here chronicled, contradicted the principle of faith. It
is the story of domestic trouble and heart-
burning, out of which arose actions which
were utterly out of keeping with the life of
simple faith in God. Through all the story
there is nevertheless manifest the consciousness of the Divine over-ruling. The interpretation of the Divine government was often at
fault, as when Rachel imagined that the son
born to Bilhah was in any sense an answer
to prayer. That answer came with the birth
of Joseph.

There were first born to Leah four sons,
Reuben, Simeon, Levi, and Judah. Then following an Eastern custom, Rachel gave her
handmaid Bilhah to Jacob, and two sons were
born, Dan and Naphtali. Then Leah, following the lead of Rachel, gave Jacob her handmaid Zilpah, and two sons were born, Gad and
Asher. There was evidently a period of
estrangement between Jacob and Leah under
the influence of Rachel. A domestic incident
of the most trivial kind was the occasion, un-

der the same influence, of reconciliation. Then there were born to Leah two sons, Issachar and Zebulun, and a daughter Dinah, who is mentioned because of the part she played in a subsequent event. Finally Joseph was born to Rachel.

This story of the birth of the children is full of interest, and reminds us that the days during which children are being born into a family are days of vital importance. The history of these sons of Jacob, so full of sadness and failure, is hardly to be wondered at, in the light of the events recorded here.

γ. *The Six Years*

At the birth of Joseph, Jacob attempted to break away from Laban. Laban, however, knew that the sojourn of Jacob with him had resulted in great gain, and for motives of absolute selfishness he was anxious to retain him; and a new arrangement was made between them, Jacob on his side being equally anxious for gain.

Laban at once attempted to make impossible the enrichment of Jacob according to this new arrangement, by setting three days' journey between the cattle ring-straked, speckled, spotted, and the rest; giving the former into the hands of his sons, and the latter into the care of Jacob. It was without question a mean and dastardly attempt to frustrate the possibility of Jacob's gaining from the compact.

The sequel shows how far he under-estimated the shrewdness of his nephew; and it is chronicled that Jacob increased exceedingly.

The procedure is not admirable on either side, but watching the movement as between two schemers, it is impossible to avoid a feeling of satisfaction that Jacob was one too many for Laban. Comparing Jacob through all this history with Abraham, it is perfectly clear that the faith of the former moved on a much lower level than that of the latter. Abraham, for instance, had been content to let the scheming Lot choose, and to give him all the advantage. Jacob, always believing in God, was yet not willing to commit these matters of worldly possession to Him.

The attempt of Laban and his sons to prevent the success of Jacob having failed, they were angry, and their dissatisfaction manifested itself in their attitude towards Jacob.

2. *The Command of God*

It was in the midst of Jacob's most con-
spicuous success, and with the shadow of the
disaffection of his uncle resting upon his pathway, that there came to him the second Divine
communication. That communication was of
the nature of a command, clear and definite, to
return immediately to the land of his fathers.
It was accompanied with words of gracious
promise, " I will be with thee."

Thus for the second time, at the moment
when it was necessary, in order that this man
might be directed into the pathway of the
Divine purpose, God appeared, disturbing him
in the very hour of his greatest success, and
turning his feet into the way of that purpose.

c. THIRD DIVINE COMMUNICATION. INDEPEND-
ENCE, AND THE CONQUERING GOD

In this section we are dealing with the great
crisis in the life of Jacob, and it falls into
three parts; the first describing the contro-
versy with Laban; the second Jacob's diplo-
macy concerning Esau; and the last, the night
of his conflict with the heavenly visitor.

1. *The Controversy with Laban*

Calling his wives to him, Jacob laid the case
before them as between their father and himself. He drew their attention to Laban's evident displeasure, called them to a recognition
of the fact that he had served Laban with all
fidelity, reminded them that Laban had many
times practised deceit toward him, and
claimed that God had not suffered Laban to
harm him.

Rachel and Leah acquiesced in Jacob's decision to depart, signifying their sense of the
change in their father; and declaring that he
looked upon them as strangers, and had
wronged them.

Thus after at least twenty years of absence,
Jacob set his face again toward home. Flee-
ing thence he had been a poor man; returning

thither he marched, the possessor of vast wealth. The same streak of cunning which had ever been manifest in his nature, is seen in the stealth with which he broke away from Laban.

Much may happen in twenty years. There is one thing, however, that can never happen. Wrongdoing cannot be undone, and Jacob was going back, as the sequel will show, with a consciousness of fear in his heart, because Esau his brother was yet alive. We shall, however, utterly fail to understand Jacob, or to do him justice, if we do not recognize the fact that the principle of faith was the inspiration of his return to his own land. He went back in obedience to a Divine command. Judging from material standards there was no reason for his going other than the suspicion and jealousy of Laban and his sons; and Jacob had already learned by experience that he was always able to outwit them. The call of God was supreme to him, notwithstanding all the cunning and deceit of his nature.

Rachel departing, had stolen the teraphim, or household gods of her father; and the sequel, notwithstanding the protestations of affection on the part of Laban, makes it perfectly clear that this was the real reason of his hot pursuit. He travelled seven days, and finally overtook Jacob in Mount Gilead. On the way God appeared to him in a dream by night, and warned him not to speak to Jacob, "either good or bad." Notwithstanding this warning he followed him, but there is no doubt it had its effect upon him.

The conference between the two men is described at length. Laban suggested that he objected to the manner of the going, and that he would fain have sent them away with rejoicings. Jacob replied that he was afraid of Laban. In all probability they were both lying. Laban's final protest was against the taking of his gods; and there followed a search for them, which through the deceit of Rachel was unsuccessful.

At last Jacob's answer flamed forth, and he found relief in telling Laban all he thought of him. The outburst of anger is most refreshing as for once at least Jacob spoke the language of honesty. He complained first of the search, which Laban had made (and in this connection it must be remembered Jacob did not know the gods were hidden); and, secondly, of the treatment that he had received from Laban, during the period he had been with him.

Laban's answer lacked the honesty of Jacob's outburst, as he affirmed his affection,

and suggested that there should be a covenant
made between them.

That covenant was entered into, and " Mizpah " ends the story. It was a heap of stones,
the emblem of suspicion, and the indication of
the fact that there were to be no further dealings between them. Mizpah was the monu-
ment of separation, erected upon the basis of
mutual suspicion. Two men called upon God,
not to ratify a comradeship, but to watch over
each on behalf of the other, as a policeman
watches a thief. Laban does not again appear
in the history, and thus the last sight we have
of him is the interesting spectacle of a man
kissing his sons and daughters, after having
wronged them through all the long years.

Thus Laban passed back to his own place,
and Jacob moved onward; and at this point
there was granted to him a vision of the angels
of God. Full of interest has been this account
of the connection between these men; but its
last message is that partnership on the ground
of selfishness, invariably issues in mutual suspicion and separation.

2. *Diplomacy concerning Esau*

There is the closest connection between the
story of Jacob's dealing with Esau and that of

his night of conflict. The whole constitutes
one of the great passages of the Bible familiar
to all the children of faith.

Jacob was returning to his own land, and
the same conflicting principles are manifest.
He was going in obedience to the distinct command of God, and yet the method of his going
was characterized by confidence in his own
ability. This is specially evident in the elabo-
rate and carefully calculated preparation he
made for his meeting with Esau. He sent messengers forward with a conciliatory message,
and they returned with the alarming report
that Esau was on his way to meet him, accompanied by four hundred men. We have no
actual evidence in the record that the purpose
of Esau was hostile, but it is evident that the
conscience of Jacob made him interpret the
advance in that way.

He immediately prepared for the meeting,
first by dividing his property into two companies, so that if Esau fell upon the one, the
other should have the opportunity of escape.
Having thus divided the property, he gave
himself to prayer, and it is impossible to read
the prayer without seeing the profounder
things in the nature of this man. It is full of
beauty. In the presence of God he declared
that he was acting in obedience to His will,

that he was conscious of his own unworthiness of all His goodness toward him; and definitely prayed for deliverance from the hand of his brother; confessing his fear on behalf of himself, and the mother with the children; ending all by pleading the promise of Jehovah.

How constantly a man in the deepest of his nature, is better than his outward actions would seem to suggest; and, moreover, how constantly the best in a man is revealed in the hour of his praying!

Having thus prayed, he prepared presents for Esau, arranging that they should reach him in relays. He hoped thus to break down his hostility, and prepare for hospitable reception.

3. *The Night of Conflict*

This return to the land was an event of great importance, and at last in the quiet stillness of the night, God appeared to Jacob in the form of a man.

He was actually alone, having sent his wives and children over the Jabbok. The long struggle of the night was that of the wrestling of the heavenly visitor with Jacob, during which God demonstrated to him his own weakness, appealing to his spiritual consciousness by a positive touch upon his physical being. In reading the story we are not to imagine for a moment that it would have been difficult for that heavenly visitor to have immediately overcome the resisting strength of Jacob. It is important rather that we should see that he was allowed to bring all his strength into play, in order that he might learn the deepest lessons.

It is certainly the story of Jacob's victory, but that victory was won in the moment when he became conscious of the superiority of the power which had laid its hand upon him; and yielding to that power with strong crying and tears, claimed and received it as his own. In that moment of yielding, with the flush of morning upon the eastern sky, there was given to this man a new name, suggestive of a new royalty. He was henceforth to be known as Israel, God-governed, rather than as Jacob, a supplanter.

The story is indeed old, and yet ever new. There are very few who have not in the course of the life of faith, spent a night of loneliness, in which they have risen through defeat into new power. The cripplings of such occasions are the crownings of men. The limp of Jacob was a life-long disability, but it was the patent of his nobility.

d. FOURTH DIVINE COMMUNICATION. COMPRO-
MISE, AND THE RESTORING GOD

The account of the fourth Divine communication consists of the story of the meeting with
Esau; an account of the first sojourn in the
land; and finally, of the definite command of
God which resulted in the return to Beth-el.

1. *The Meeting with Esau*

In the flush of the new morning Jacob went
forward to the meeting with Esau. Esau advanced with four hundred men, according to
the report of the messengers that Jacob had
first seen.

Jacob went to meet him, following upon the
droves of cattle which he had sent forward, as
presents to Esau. In his approach to his
brother, he himself led the way, followed immediately by his handmaids and their children, and finally by Rachel and Joseph. How
strange a mixture this man was is made evident here again. It is clearly to be seen that
a fear of his brother still lurked in his heart,
and there is a touch of nobleness discernible
in his first going forward to meet Esau, having
set his loved ones behind in three companies.

His love of Rachel is here again manifest as he put her in the last company, so that if peradventure Esau should still meet him in anger and fall upon the first, she might have the better opportunity of escape.

The chief interest of the study, however, centres in the attitude of Esau. Instead of an angry man, Jacob met a brother. While we have in a previous consideration recognized the fact that there is nothing in the text to warrant us in believing that Esau's defence was characterized by hostility, it is nevertheless more than probable that such was the case. but God, Who Holds in His own power the disposing of all hearts, while manifestly He had been dealing with Jacob by the brook, had in all probability unconsciously to Esau, prepared his heart for the meeting with his brother. After twenty years of separation, when these men came together, they did so with affection and with emotion.

It is an interesting illustration of the fact that in proportion as a man finds his way into the will of God, he finds his way to a pathway prepared for him. All Jacob's preparations for the appeasing of Esau would evidently have been of no avail, for he did not desire the presents; but God had solved the difficulty for the man who had been brought into submission to Him, in the long struggle of the lonely night.

In the conference between the brothers, the children of Jacob, and his wives were presented to Esau; he accepted the present of Jacob under pressure; but Jacob emphatically, although courteously, refused any help from Esau.

They separated, Esau journeying to Seir, and Jacob a little distance on to Succoth, where he halted for a while. The making of booths for his cattle was in itself a suggestive action, for they were for purposes of safety against marauders, rather than for protection from the weather.

2. *The Dwelling in the Land*

How long Jacob remained at Succoth we are not told, but moving from there, he crossed the Jordan, and encamped in the neighbourhood of the city of Shechem. There he bought a parcel of ground, and erected an altar. This tarrying at Shechem was undoubtedly a mistake. The word spoken to him by Jehovah in Paddan-aram, commanding him to return, had been quite explicit, " Return unto the land of thy fathers, and to thy kindred "; and there can be no doubt that he ought at once to have continued his journey at least to Beth-el, the place where God had first appeared to him, and made His covenant with him; and in all probability the full terms of the command intended that he should have passed immediately to Hebron, where Isaac was still living. There is nothing more perilous than to stop short of the place to which God is calling, and the story which follows is that of a sad and tragic reaping from this halt.

Dinah at this time could not have been more than a mere girl; and the record makes it perfectly clear that her departure from the camp of her people was simply due to curiosity, and her desire to see the daughters of the land, that is, to observe the habits of the women of another country and another people. It was during this escapade that she was seen by Shechem, the son of the prince of the land; and if we may read into the ancient story much that we know of human nature in more modern times, it is easy to follow the movement of this fresh and artless girl through frivolity to defilement.

Jacob heard the story, but maintained silence concerning it.

It is evident that this man Shechem had genuinely fallen in love with the girl, from the earnest suit he and his father paid to Jacob for her hand.

The story of the action of the sons of Jacob is, as to the method adopted, as evil as that of the failure of their sister. They made to these men a deceitful proposition, suggesting that if the whole of them would submit to the rite of circumcision, their sister should be given to Shechem to wife. The devotion of Shechem to Dinah, and the great influence of his father and himself over his people, is evidenced by the fact that the whole of the citizens of Shechem submitted to the rite. Then the cruelty of Simeon and Levi manifested itself in their murder of these men, while all the sons of Jacob shared in the spoiling of the city.

The complaint of Jacob was utterly unworthy of a man of faith. It breathed a spirit of selfish fear from first to last. There was no word of jealousy for the honour of God, and no word of rebuke at this point for the cruelty of his sons. He came to the consciousness of that later, as his final words concerning them will reveal. At the moment he was simply filled with cowardly fear. The moment in which faith ceases to be the simple principle of life, self is enthroned; and instead of the calm courage which is the result of obedient faith, there ensues the miserable fear of personal suffering.

In the answer of his sons to his fear there

is a tone of healthy protest against the wrong
which Shechem had done their sister. That,
however, was no justification for the method
of punishment which they had adopted. This
whole story constitutes a startling revelation
of how the fruits of a man's disobedience may
be gathered in the history of his family. How
often, alas! children have been harmed incal-
culably, because parents, while believing in
God, have yet tarried at some Shechem of
worldly advantage, instead of centring all
their interests around Beth-el and the altar.

3. *The Command of God*

The background of conditions which we
have considered throws into clear relief the
meaning of the Divine intervention at this
point. God does not abandon His children to
the evil circumstances which result from their
own folly. Jacob was commanded to leave
Shechem, to go to Beth-el and dwell there,
to make there an altar to God; and the command was joined to the reminder that there
God appeared to him when he fled from the
face of Esau his brother. Thus the fourth
Divine communication was the means of his
restoration to the pathway of the Divine purpose.

e. FIFTH DIVINE COMMUNICATION.   OBEDIENCE,
AND THE REWARDING GOD

The response of Jacob to the command to return to Beth-el was immediate, and led up to the fifth communication.

1. *Purification*

He called upon his own household, and all who were associated with him, to put away strange gods, and to mark the purification of the camp by ceremonial cleansing and changing. He distinctly declared that his purpose was to erect at Beth-el an altar unto God. The obedience of the people associated with him was prompt, as they handed over to him their strange gods and their earrings, both of which in all probability were spoils resulting from the sack of Shechem.

2. *Obedience*

Having thus purified themselves, they took their journey to Beth-el, protected by the terror of God which rested upon the cities through which they passed. Arrived at Beth-el, Jacob erected his altar, calling it El-beth-el or the God of Beth-el, or more literally still, the God of the house of God.

Here Deborah died and was buried. It will be remembered that she came from Laban's country with Rebekah, when in response to the call of Eliezer, she journeyed to become the bride of Isaac. This incidental reference to her would suggest that Rebekah was dead ere Jacob returned into the land, but that on his return he was joined by Deborah for the sake of his mother.

3. *The Appearing of God*

It was in this hour of obedience that there came to Jacob the fifth and final communication of God, so far as his personal history is concerned. In the subsequent history God spoke to him again, but the word had special reference to his sons, and therefore is not included in the account of the dealings of God with Jacob himself. The name Israel was again pronounced. It would seem as though Jacob had never entered into the experience of the blessing won by the Jabbok during the time that he tarried at Succoth, and then in the neighbourhood of Shechem. In that night of wrestling the vision had come to him, but it had not been translated into victory in the details of life.

How often this is so! In some great crisis

of revelation a larger life is seen, its laws
appreciated, its claim intellectually yielded to,
while yet it is not wrought out into the details
of life; and sometimes its greatest value is
only gained through a subsequent experience
of failure.

By this second declaration his right to the
name Israel was ratified, and there immediately followed a ratification of the Divine
covenant. It is full of interest to notice that
this ratification of the covenant commenced
with the declaration of a special name
of God. It is the name El Shaddai,
which He had first used to Abraham in
connection with the changing of his name.
It signifies that God is all-sufficient for the
needs of those who put their trust in Him. In
the night of wrestling the name of Jacob was
changed to that of Israel, but when he asked
the name of God he was not answered. Now
that in the pathway of obedience he had found
his way into a fuller experience of what his
new name suggested, the name which signifies
the absolute sufficiency of God was that by
which He declared Himself to him.

This declaration was followed by a command to be fruitful and to multiply; and the
promise was made that a nation, and a company of nations, should be born of him, that

kings should come out of his loins, and that
the land should be given to him and to his
seed.

4. *The Response of Jacob*

To this revelation Jacob responded by the
erection of a pillar, and the pouring out of a
drink-offering. It was upon this occasion that
he named the place Beth-el. It will be remembered that on his previous sojourn here, on
his way to Paddan-aram, he had said, " This
is none other than Beth-el, and this is the gate
of heaven," but it was now that he definitely
changed the name from Luz to Beth-el.

5. *The Death of Rachel*

Immediately following this experience
Jacob passed through the darkness of the
greatest personal sorrow of his life. On the
journey Rachel died in giving birth to one
whom she named, The son of my sorrow, but
whom his father called, The son of the right
hand. She was buried at Bethlehem, and
Israel continued his journey.

II. OF THE FAMILY

We now come to that section of the book of Genesis in which we see the movement toward the regeneration of the family. It is a striking fact that the main impression of this whole section is that of the corruption of the family of Jacob. In the midst of it, however, there is the wonderful story of the eldest born son of his beloved Rachel, maintaining his purity in the midst of the most trying circumstances, and against fierce temptation; and thus becoming a link in God's chain of movement toward the advent of the One through Whom the word spoken to Abraham should be fulfilled, that in him all the families of the earth should be blessed.

This section falls into three parts, the first being preliminary; the second giving us a picture of Joseph at home and in exile; and the third telling the appalling story of Judah's corruption.

i. PRELIMINARY

This preliminary section briefly records the sin of Reuben, in consequence of which the birthright was taken from him, and given to Joseph (1 Chron. v. 1).

Then follows a list of the sons of Jacob; the account of the death of Isaac; and the generations of Esau.

This record of the generations of Esau is at once startling and solemn as a revelation of the prolific progeny of that profane person Esau. Faster than the seed of promise, multiplied the sons of the flesh. The most interesting aspect is, of course, that of the relation to Israel. One brief and pregnant sentence in the chapter flashes its light along the coming centuries. " Of Esau is Edom." What Edom meant to Israel the subsequent history reveals. Though personally Jacob escaped the anger of his brother, the great harvests resulting from his deceit were reaped in the after-years.

Oh these harvests of the centuries! When will men learn the awful and stupendous greatness of life? The deed of good or evil, of truth or falsehood, done to-day, is not ended, though it is done. There is, indeed, nothing small. This sense of infinite values touching minutest details is lost to men generally, and is only restored with the bestowment of age-abiding life, which, among other things, is the consciousness of this very fact that the things of the passing moment are irrevocably linked to the undying ages.

ii. Joseph at Home and in Exile

From this point, though Jacob appears
more than once again in the sacred narrative,
the history centres round Joseph; and in many
respects there is no more remarkable figure
upon the page of Old Testament history. In
the present section he is seen as the object of
his father's love, a love which may certainly
be accounted for by the fact that he was the
firstborn of Rachel, but which was also due to
the ingenuous simplicity of his disposition,
and the strong integrity of his character.
There are three movements in the picture; the
first being that of the home life; the second
that of his dreams; and the third that of his
betrayal by his brethren.

a. THE HOME LIFE

Jacob was now dwelling in the old home-
stead, in the land of his father's sojournings;
and there Joseph, being seventeen years of
age, was occupied in feeding the flocks, in company with the sons of Bilhah and of Zilpah.
His father's love for him was specially indicated by the coat which he wore. The word
employed for " coat " suggests the long-sleeved
garment which was worn by the heir, a posi-

tion which Joseph occupied by the will of his father, after the sin of Reuben, already referred to. In consequence of this he was hated of his brethren.

b. THE DREAMS

Naturally imaginative and romantic, and given to dreams, God through this avenue suggested to him his coming position and power. With simple artlessness he told the dreams to his brethren. The character of Joseph, as subsequently revealed, makes it impossible to believe that he had ulterior motives in so doing. The construction which his brethren placed upon them was undoubtedly the true one; but they arrived at the conclusion as the result of the position he occupied among them by the appointment of his father; and their interpretation of his feeling by their own jealousies.

c. THE BETRAYAL

The story of his betrayal is graphically told, and needs no detailed repetition. Sent by his father to seek them, he travelled to Shechem, and on to Dothan. They entered into a conspiracy to slay him, but Reuben, the one most implicated in Jacob's preference for Joseph, interfered to deliver him out of their hands, proposing that he should be cast into a pit from which he intended presently to rescue him, and send him back to his father. Having done this, unknown to Reuben, they sold him to a company of Ishmaelites, who carried him to Egypt. The picture of Jacob in his grief is very real. In the meantime Joseph was sold into slavery, and came into the house of Potiphar, an officer of Pharaoh's.

Surveying this story from the standpoint of the Divine purpose, it is a simple instance of the over-ruling of the wrath and malice of men by God in purposes of mercy and grace.

iii. Judah's Corruption

The story of the corruption of Judah immediately follows, and again is so graphically told as to need no detailed exposition. It carries its own lessons of the frailty of human nature, and of the far-reaching effects of sin.

Its placing at this point in the history is suggestive and full of importance. So far the setting forth of the first movements in the working of regeneration have been almost exclusively occupied with individuals. There is gradually emerging into view the larger

purpose of the regeneration of the family and
of society. The conditions which made possible the sin of Judah, and that sin itself,
reveal the necessity for another new departure.
There is a marked tendency towards the corruption of the chosen people by unhallowed
intercourse with the peoples of the land. If
there had been no Divine over-ruling, and
they had been left to themselves, in all
probability the chosen seed would have been
utterly corrupted, and the very purposes of
regeneration through them frustrated.

While Judah was thus sinning, Joseph was
already in Egypt. Glancing ahead for a
moment, we see the purpose of his being there
in the economy of God. Preparation was already being made for the segregation of the
chosen people for a long period, in which their
separation from or mixture with other people
was secured by the rigid exclusiveness of the
Egyptians. Another and an almost startling
value of this terrible story of corruption is
that it introduces to us Tamar and Perez, who
are both named in the genealogical table of
our Lord, which is found in the Gospel of
Matthew.

III. OF SOCIETY

We now begin the history of Joseph in Egypt which is so full of interest, dealing as it does with the Divine method in the regeneration of a Society threatened with corruption, and leading on to the movement toward the regeneration of national life. This division, which is the last of the book in detail, falls into two main parts, the first dealing with the preparation in Egypt for the coming of the children of Israel; and the second with the segregation of Israel in order to the accomplishment of Divine purpose.

i. PREPARATION IN EGYPT

The account of the preparation in Egypt is centred in Joseph, and falls into three sections; the first dealing with Joseph in slavery; the second with Joseph in power; and the third with Joseph and his brethren.

a. JOSEPH IN SLAVERY

The story of Joseph in slavery deals with his success; his temptation; and his imprisonment.

1. *His Success*

Through the malice of his brethren he had
been sold into slavery, and we now see him in
the house of Potiphar. Here, at the very commencement of the record of his life and work
in Egypt, the statement is made which gives
us the secret of all his wonderful success, " Jehovah was with him "; and immediately we
are impressed by the fact that to that statement another is linked, " his master saw that
Jehovah was with him." In these statements
we have the picture of a man in circumstances
full of difficulty, because they were those
which are always calculated to degrade life.
He was a slave, held by another man as his
property. Nevertheless in these very circumstances he so lived as to demonstrate to his
master the fact that he was a man having
communion with God. This conviction in the
mind of Potiphar resulted in the promotion
of Joseph to a position of trust. While it is
perfectly true that godly men must suffer persecution sooner or later, it is equally true that
the life of simple godliness commands the
respect and trust even of ungodly men.

2. *His Temptation*

The story of his temptation is graphically told. It was a temptation subtle and fierce, presenting itself as it did through one who was supposed to be infinitely his superior in social position. His quiet and heroic victory is a revelation of the strength of a man who lives in habitual communion with God, even under stress of temptation which is at once subtle, sudden, and strong. Having failed to lead him into sin, his temptress became his slanderer.

3. *His Imprisonment*

a. The Favour of Jehovah

Again Joseph found his circumstances changed as Potiphar sent him to prison. Immediately the same affirmation is made, as at the commencement, " Jehovah was with him "; and the fact was manifest in the prison as in the household of Potiphar, with practically the same result of promotion to a position of trust. The story is a radiant revelation of the wonderful truth that God is always loyal to the man who is loyal to Him. Whether in slavery or in prison, in prosperity or in adversity, Jehovah was with Joseph, and in that sacred and gracious fellowship he was triumphant over circumstances.

β. *The Dreams of Prisoners*

The methods of God are generally those of the over-ruling of the simple things of life. There is no study more fascinating in the Divine Oracles, or in human experience, than that of the wonderful mosaic of the Divine government. There are no forces nor facts upon which God does not lay His hand in quiet strength and majesty, and make them tributary to the accomplishment of His purpose. He now wrought in the case of Joseph with great certainty and exactness, through the uncertain and inexact medium of dreams. Prisoners of Pharaoh were troubled in the night, and through such troubling God proceeded in the carrying out of His designs.

Soon after the imprisonment of Joseph the chief butler and the chief baker at Pharaoh's court in some way offended their lord, and in consequence were committed to the prison. The captain of the guard put them under the care of Joseph. After a period of imprisonment they dreamed dreams which filled them with sadness. Joseph inquired the reason of their sadness, and they told him their dreams.

In this connection he is still seen as a man entirely dependent upon his God, in that he declared to them that interpretation belonged to Him. In that dependence he interpreted their dreams, foretelling the restoration of the butler to power, and the condemnation of the baker to death.

Three days after this, his interpretation was vindicated, and his prophecy fulfilled.

There is a beautifully human touch in the request which Joseph made to the butler, " Have me in thy remembrance when it shall be well with thee "; showing that a man may be living in true fellowship with God, triumphing in many ways over the limitations of his position, and yet conscious of the irksomeness of restrictions which, on the human side, he has no right to be enduring. He was conscious of the limitation of his life, and evidently sighed, as every healthy man must do, for liberty, and the larger possibilities which would come therewith.

There is another human touch, quite as natural, in the words, " chief butler . . . forgat him." How good it is to remember that God did not forget him.

b. JOSEPH IN POWER

We now pass to the consideration of how, under the government of God, Joseph came into the position of power in Egypt; and the section may be divided into three parts, dealing in turn with Joseph's interpretation, exaltation, and administration.

1. *Interpretation*

Still the Divine activity proceeded, this time through the dreaming king and the remembering butler. Pharaoh was troubled by his strange dreams concerning the kine and the corn, and the more so, because neither the magicians of Egypt nor the wise men could interpret to him the meaning of these dreams.

It was at this time, two years having passed away, that the butler remembered Joseph; and he confessed to Pharaoh his fault, recounting his experience in the prison, and how that Joseph had accurately interpreted, both his own dream, and that of the chief baker.

Pharaoh immediately sent for him, and as he stood before the king, he maintained the same attitude of dependence upon God, boldly proclaiming that dependence. In answer to the king's statement that he had heard that

when Joseph heard a dream he could interpret
it, he replied, " It is not in me: God shall give
Pharaoh an answer of peace." The king then
told his dreams to Joseph; and without hesi-
tation, and with great clearness, he interpreted
their meaning to him, adding to his interpretation his advice that he should appoint officers
and conserve the plenty of the first seven
years, in order to supply the need of the
second seven. It is noticeable how definitely
Joseph announced that the character of the
years was within the government of God, and
that the dreams had been given to Pharaoh
by God.

2. *Exaltation*

The dreams being thus interpreted, Pharaoh
immediately recognized in Joseph " a man in
whom the spirit of God is "; a very remarkable description as coming from the lips of
this man.

This recognition was followed by the appointment of Joseph to the first place of power
in the kingdom, next to that of the king himself, with the clear declaration of the fact that
the appointment was made because the king
recognized that he had spoken under the direction of God.

This appointment was followed by the conferring upon Joseph of the insignia of office; as Pharaoh placed his own signet-ring upon the hand of Joseph, arrayed him in fine linen, placed about his neck a gold chain, and caused him to ride in the second chariot, while the couriers proclaimed him and called upon the people to make obeisance before him.

He conferred upon him the name Zaphenath-paneah, which means Abundance-of-life, and gave him to wife Asenath, who was the daughter of an Egyptian priest in On, which was the city of the sun, the great educational centre in Egypt. These actions on the part of Pharaoh were of the nature of favours conferred upon Joseph.

3. *Administration*

Thus, when only thirty years of age, Joseph stood in the position of practically supreme power in Egypt, and commenced that masterly administration of affairs which resulted not only in the succour of Egypt, but in the material salvation of his own kin; and in their being brought into the place of separation from corruption, and prepared for emergence into national life in fulfilment of the council of Jehovah.

During the seven years of plenty there were born to him his two sons, Manasseh and Ephraim.

Thus the story of the activity of Jehovah through this man Joseph moves forward. In slavery, in prison, at the court of the king, Jehovah was with His servant. This fact was recognized in turn by Potiphar, the chief keeper of the prison, and Pharaoh himself; and in each case the result was that Joseph was placed in a position of power, in the house of his master, in the prison of his confinement, and in the realm of the king.

True godliness will manifest itself. Nothing but genuine godliness ever commands respect.

Thus the great regenerative movement proceeded, and things were surely developing toward the accomplishment of the Divine purpose. One of the chief values of these Old Testament histories is the revelation of these underlying principles. This story of Joseph is not merely that of a condition of affairs which obtained millenniums ago. In all essential values it is a story of the hour in which we live. In the midst of the movements of our own age, though men may be utterly un-

conscious of it, the Divine purpose is being
wrought out through human history; and all
forces, material, mental, and moral, are being
compelled to contribute toward the consum-
mation upon which the heart of God is set.

c. JOSEPH AND HIS BRETHREN

The seven years of plenty having run their course, those of famine immediately followed in accordance with the prediction of Joseph. Through his executive ability, Egypt was provided with corn sufficient, not only for its own needs, but to enable it to supply other peoples. Under this necessity his brethren came down from Canaan to procure corn from Egypt; and the account of his meeting with them after more than twenty years falls into two parts; the first dealing with their first visit; and the second with their second.

1. *The First Visit*

The account of their first visit to Egypt tells how ten were sent by their father, of their meeting with their brother Joseph, and of how nine returned to Jacob.

α. The Sending of the Ten

The words of Jacob to his sons, " Why do ye look one upon another? " make it evident that the famine in Canaan was severe, and had produced distress there. In sending them to Egypt he kept Benjamin by him. Evidently his sorrow over the loss of Joseph was yet fresh in his heart, and he was not sure of the trustworthiness of his older sons.

β. The Meeting with Joseph

At last, in fulfilment of the dream of long ago, these brethren of Joseph bowed down in his presence. Immediately recognizing them, he treated them as strangers, and "spake roughly to them," demanding whence they came. On receiving their answer that they had come from the land of Canaan to buy food, he charged them with being spies. In the course of their answer, when questioned about themselves, they said, "We are . . . twelve brethren . . . one is not." Even though they did not know Joseph, they were conscious of their guilt. It would seem as though the wrong done to their brother long ago had haunted them through the years, the sense of it recurring with new force in any hour of danger. Though they had no idea that the Egyptian governor was their brother, the memory of the sin sprang vividly up when they found themselves in peril of complications.

Upon their confession that they were twelve, Joseph instituted no inquiry as to the

one to whom they referred when they said, he
" is not " ; but demanded that they should dis-
prove the charge he had made against them,
by producing their youngest brother. He cast
them into prison for three days, at the end
of which time he granted them permission to
go, carrying corn with them, providing that
they left one of their number as hostage for
their reappearance with their youngest
brother.

Of course, not knowing that he could understand their language, they talked together in
his presence of the wrong they had done to
Joseph, and declared their belief that their
present position was a judgment on them for
their sin.

Hearing them thus engaged in conversation,
all the memories of the bygone days came back
vividly to Joseph, and he was moved to tears.

He retained Simeon as hostage, and sent
them on their way, having commanded that
the money which they had brought should be
placed in their sacks.

γ. *The Return of the Nine*

Thus nine of them returned to their father
Jacob. Discovering their money in their
sacks on the way, they were filled with even

greater consternation, being unable to understand what it portended.

Arrived in Canaan they carefully reported to their father all that had passed in Egypt.

When he heard that the governor had demanded the presence of Benjamin, he broke out into a wailing rebuke of his sons, declaring, " all these things are against me."

This was not the language of faith, and yet surely no one can criticize him, for the outlook was dark enough. Had he been a man of simpler faith, perchance he might have been able to say, " all things work together for good." This was actually so, for those things which seemed to be against him were working together for the restoration to him of his long-lost son, and for the moving forward toward completion of those gracious purposes for which he and his father stood. We may surely learn, as we listen to the wail of Jacob, that it is never wise to measure the facts of any hour by the limitations of our own vision.

Reuben offered that his two sons should remain with Jacob as guarantee of the safety of Benjamin, but the old man was obdurate, and declared that he would not spare him, seeing that his brother was dead, and he only was left. In these words his abiding love for Rachel is clearly manifest.

2. *The Second Visit*

The story of the second visit is longer, and even more full of interest. It may be divided into seven parts, dealing respectively with the consultation with Israel, the return to Egypt, the departure from Egypt, the arrest and return, the revealing interview with Joseph, the action of Pharaoh, and the return to Israel.

α. *The Consultation with Israel*

The continuation of the famine pressed hardly upon the Hebrews, and made it necessary that there should be another journey to Egypt to procure corn. All the old characteristics of Jacob manifest themselves in this story.

Judah reminded his father seriously and plainly that the governor in Egypt had declared that they should not see his face unless their brother were with them; and told him that they were willing to go on condition that Benjamin accompanied them, and on no other condition.

Then the cunning of Israel was manifested in his question, " Wherefore dealt ye so ill with me, as to tell the man whether ye had yet a brother? " They all replied that they had been asked the definite question, which was not strictly true, for they themselves had declared to Joseph "thy servants are twelve brethren . . . and behold, the youngest is this day with our father."

Judah again urged his father to consent to the going of Benjamin, promising to stand surety for his safe restoration.

And once again the old spirit manifested itself in his arrangement to send a present, and so to appease the man. If things were against him as he had declared, he had not wholly lost confidence in his own ability to manipulate them to his own advantage. Thus all unconsciously, he was revealing himself by his perpetual method of attempting to deal with men. He always seemed to think that the great end was to gain something, and evidently he believed that this was the motive of the Egyptian governor, and that, therefore, he might be bribed into complacency. How often we but reveal ourselves in our estimates of others!

β. The Return to Egypt

The picture of Joseph here is full of beauty. He was now, so far as worldly position was concerned, one of the greatest of men, occupying a place of honour, and even of international influence. Yet the springs of his true life were not dried up. His emotional nature was quick and active. This in itself is a sure evidence that he was a man living in fellowship with God. The perils of powerful positions are in some senses subtler and more mighty than those of slavery or of prison. Advancement, with the greater ease and more luxuriant circumstances attendant upon it, too often serve to deaden the finer emotions of the soul. Even in such circumstances, however, a man is safe if Jehovah is with him.

Having officially received them, he commanded his steward that they were to be taken to his house, and that a feast was to be prepared for them.

This action on his part filled them with apprehension, and they feared that it was a trap to capture them as bondmen. They appealed to the steward, declaring the honesty of their coming and their intention. He immediately reassured them, declaring that he had their money, and that the treasure which they had found in their sacks was the gift of God to them.

At the hour of Joseph's return he received them kindly, and inquired after their father. When he saw Benjamin, his heart was full, and he left them and entered into his own chamber and wept. The rush of emotion which drove him into secrecy for weeping was as surely evidence of his true greatness, as were the statesmanlike qualities which had served him in the administration of the affairs of Egypt in the hour of difficulty. It is to be noticed that at this feast there was a clear line of separation between the Egyptians and the Hebrews, because the Egyptians considered it an abomination to eat with those who were shepherds. All this was part of the Divine plan for the separation of the Hebrew people, and will be seen more clearly as we proceed.

γ. *The Departure from Egypt*

After the feast, by the command of Joseph, their sacks were filled with food, and again their money fastened in the mouth of the sacks, while his own silver cup was placed in the sack of Benjamin. In the morning of the following day they started on their homeward journey. Criticisms of Joseph's actions with regard to the placing of money and his cup in the sacks of his brethren have sometimes been offered. Surely such criticisms, to put the matter in the mildest form, reveal a lack of humour on the part of the critics. The story is really natural and beautiful. Such methods are only possible to a man who retains the heart of a boy. Joseph was deliberately preparing for a dramatic ending, and one can imagine his quiet enjoyment of the temporary perturbation of his brethren, as he moved forward toward the moment when he would reveal himself, and be able to pour out upon them all the pent-up love of his heart.

δ. The Arrest and Return

They were quickly followed by Joseph's steward, and in spite of their protestations of innocence, their sacks were searched; and on the discovery of the silver cup in the sack of Benjamin, they were taken back to the city.

ε. The revealing Interview with Joseph

Again in the presence of Joseph these men made obeisance, in fulfilment of the dream of his youth.

There is a nobleness and a beauty in the plea of Judah on behalf of his father. In the background of his eloquent appeal there was evidently a keen consciousness of the sin of the past, and a desire so far as might be to atone, or at least to prevent any further catastrophe darkening the last days of the old man. With a splendid devotion to this high purpose, he asked to be allowed to take the place of Benjamin, in the mouth of whose sack the cup of the governor had been found.

At last the moment for which Joseph had been planning arrived, and he determined in this hour of their greatest perplexity and distress to make himself known to them. A man of so great a heart could not do so without betraying his emotion, and his first action was that of commanding that every man other than his brethren should leave his presence. He then broke out into loud lamentation, which even the Egyptians of the house of Pharaoh heard. How astonished his brethren must have been, seeing that as yet they could not know the reason of his tears. In a voice broken with emotion he at last said, " I am Joseph; doth my father yet live? " It is not to be wondered at that they could not answer him, and he then more carefully declared that he indeed was Joseph their brother, whom they had sold into Egypt.

In this account of Joseph's revelation of himself to his brothers, the chief value for us is to be found in his recognition of the government of God in the history of the past. He distinctly declared to them, " It was not you that sent me hither, but God." This capacity for ignoring secondary causes is one of the surest signs of greatness, but it is only possible to men of faith. Yet how great it enables a man to be! Recognizing the Divine over-ruling, Joseph was able to forget the action of his brethren, when they sold him into slavery. The same power was manifest long after in Paul, who, speaking after the manner of men, was a prisoner of Nero, never referred to himself as such, but always described himself as a prisoner of Jesus Christ. Superlatively and finally was this manifested in Christ, when He said to Pilate, " Thou wouldest have no power against Me, except it were given thee from above." It is a consciousness only possible in the life of habitual communion, the condition of such com-

munion is purity of heart. " Blessed are the
pure in heart, for they shall see God," over-
ruling all circumstances.

Having thus declared his conviction concerning his presence in Egypt, he commanded
them to depart, and to bring Jacob back with
them. The picture of Joseph and Benjamin,
locked in each other's embrace, is full of
beauty. Having also embraced his brethren
it is said, " And after that his brethren talked
with him." The sure evidences of his love set
them free from fear, and made communion possible.

ζ. *The Action of Pharaoh*

The importance of the position Joseph occupied in Egypt is clearly seen in the attitude
of Pharaoh toward his father and his brethren,
who, when it was reported to him, " Joseph's
brethren are come," was pleased; and commanded Joseph to send for the whole company of his own people, and lay before them
the good of the land of Egypt. He moreover
instructed Joseph to send wagons in which
to bring the whole company down.

η. *The Return to Israel*

Thus, accompanied by the caravans of
Egypt, and laden with presents, they returned

to their father. Very significant was the word Joseph addressed to them as they departed, " See that ye fall not out by the way." He evidently knew them well.

With what peculiar joy old Jacob must have heard the news that his son was alive! Though at first his heart fainted, yet his spirit revived, and there is a beautiful tenderness in his words, " It is enough; Joseph my son is yet alive: I will go and see him before I die."

Thus he was beginning to discover that the things which he had declared to be against him, were really for him, under the government of his covenant-keeping God. How good a thing it is for all of us that when our faith wavers, God does not change His mind or purpose concerning us, but moves right on in infinite Love toward the final good. How much of feverish unrest should we be spared if these stories of the past might only teach us to repose our confidence in God, rather than in circumstances, and quietly to wait His time!

ii. SEGREGATION OF ISRAEL

The story of the going down of Jacob and his sons into Egypt must be read in the light of that whole Divine movement which we are attempting to keep in mind in the study of this book, for it is distinctly a part of the programme of God. It may be divided into two parts, that first dealing with Joseph and his family; and secondly that dealing with Joseph, his sons, and his father.

a. JOSEPH AND HIS FAMILY

The section dealing with the family of Joseph and their coming into Egypt falls into two parts, the first telling the story of the coming from Canaan; and the second giving an account of their settlement in Goshen.

1. *The Coming from Canaan*

The first stage of the journey of Israel was to Beer-sheba, where he offered sacrifices to God, and where God appeared to him, and charged him not to be afraid, making him a threefold promise. The first note of that promise was that He would make of him a great nation there, that is, in Egypt. How much lay concealed in that word, Jacob in all probability, did not understand. To him the promise would be interpreted as meaning great in numbers, and that it had such intention there can be no doubt; but history shows that it meant far more, for through discipline and suffering, the nation was to be made great in other ways than numerically. God only reveals to men at any given time so much as they are able to bear.

Yet in case any fear should come to the heart of His servant, He promised him secondly, "I will go down with thee"; and finally, "I will . . . bring thee up." It is interesting to note that on this occasion God still spoke to him by his old name, Jacob; recognizing that he had not even yet experimentally entered into all that was in the will of God for him; and indicating the fact that notwithstanding his failure to realize all, God would still continue to guide.

Having thus sacrificed to God, and received his message, Jacob rose up; and accompanied by his sons, their little ones, and their wives, they journeyed in the wagons which Pharaoh had provided, into Egypt.

Next in order we have a full list of those who thus went down with Jacob into Egypt.

Three-score and six actually accompanied

him. Joseph and his two sons, who were also counted as belonging to the house of Israel, were already in the land; and Jochebed, the mother of Moses, born after arrival, was probably also counted in the seventy of the total.[1]

Judah was sent forward to show the way to Goshen, where Joseph met them; and the meeting between himself and his father was a glad one.

Joseph's charge to his brethren in view of their presentation to Pharaoh was most careful, and was undoubtedly part of the Divine purpose for the segregation of the people. He charged them to be careful to declare themselves to Pharaoh as shepherds. This would ensure the maintenance of the line of separation between the Egyptians and the Hebrews, because " every shepherd is an abomination unto the Egyptians."

The picture of Jacob before Pharaoh is characterized by a striking dignity. One of the most interesting lines of study in the history of Jacob is the way in which he alternated between faith and fear. When presented to Pharaoh the deepest side of his nature was manifested, that of his faith in God, and his

[1] The reference in Acts vii. 14 to seventy-five souls would include some of his kindred, who were not " out of his loins " (Gen. xlvi. 26).

consciousness of his own position in the Divine economy. This was seen in his patriarchal blessing of Pharaoh. He was receiving from Pharaoh a place in which to dwell, and yet he pronounced a blessing upon him. The less is ever blessed of the greater, and there would seem to have been in the action of Jacob a consciousness of Divine over-ruling inspiring his action. This is the true attitude of the people of faith. They ever recognize that they are channels of blessing to those with whom they come in contact. Such consciousness, however, does not create the tone of officious superiority, but rather inspires the desire to confer blessing. The true dignity of a godly people amongst ungodly men is that of the bestowment of blessing, and never that of the assumption of secular authority.

2. *The Settlement in Goshen*

The formal presentation to Pharaoh being over, Israel and his sons were given a possession in the land, and Joseph made provision for their need.

In this section we have a glimpse of Joseph as the administrator of Egyptian affairs. His policy must be judged by the times in which he lived. We need only notice in passing that it was a policy which ensured at once the interests of the king, of the nation, and of the people themselves. It was one of unification and consolidation. The point of particular interest for us is the bearing of it on the history of Israel. By the centralization of authority in one head, he precluded the possibility of the harassment of the Hebrew people by the Egyptians, and the rivalries of petty princes. Of course, it is equally true that by this very action he made possible what subsequently happened, the enslaving of the whole people by the will of the supreme Pharaoh. Thus again the hand of God was seen operating through Egyptian policy for the immediate safety of His people; and ultimately for the long discipline of slavery and suffering through which they were to pass.

Thus settled in Goshen, the Hebrew people entered upon a period of prosperity. In this section it is again interesting to notice the interchange of names made use of. In referring to the whole of the people it is declared that Israel dwelt in the land of Egypt, and it is said of them, " they gat them possessions . . . were fruitful . . . multiplied." Referring to the man it is said that Jacob lived in the land of Egypt; but when the reference is to his coming death, he is described as Israel. Thus the conflicting forces within him are manifest. He was still Jacob, the schemer and the supplanter, even though he dwelt in the land which he possessed through no plan of his own, but wholly by the government of God. It would seem as though never until the end did he fully realize his Israel life, and in this connection it is interesting to notice that the writer of the letter to the Hebrews only speaks of his faith as manifest, when dying, he blessed his sons, and worshipped; and even then he speaks of him as Jacob.

In the present section both his faith and his fears are manifest; his faith in that he chose to be buried with his fathers; his fear in that he made Joseph swear so to bury him.

b. JOSEPH, HIS SONS, AND HIS FATHER

In this section we have three divisions dealing respectively with Jacob's adoption of Ephraim and Manasseh; Jacob's prophecy concerning his sons; and Jacob's passing and burial.

1. *Jacob's Adoption of Ephraim and Manasseh*

Here again we are arrested by the interchange of names. Jacob was sick, but hearing that Joseph was coming to see him, it was Israel who strengthened himself and sat upon the bed. And yet again Jacob spoke. In what he said to Joseph concerning his sons there was still evident the planning of the schemer, who in his own foresight would make arrangements for the retention of Joseph and his seed within the covenant of promise.

And yet how wonderfully the Divine overruling is seen even in this matter, for in this determination of Jacob to adopt Ephraim and Manasseh, provision was made for the redemption of Joseph from Egypt. He had married an Egyptian woman, and occupied a place of peculiar power in Egypt. What more likely than that his sons would be brought up

as Egyptians? The action of Jacob claimed
these boys as his own, and thus retained the
succession of Joseph within the border of that
people whom God had created, and was preparing for the carrying out of His own purpose.

He first declared to Joseph the promise
which God Almighty had made to him, that
he and his seed should have the land of Canaan
for an everlasting possession. He then
claimed the two sons born to Joseph before
his own arrival in Egypt, declaring that the
other sons of Joseph should remain to possess
their inheritance in their own land.

Very touching was his reference to Rachel,
as he talked to Joseph, showing how she still
occupied the supreme place in his affection.

In all the remainder of this particular story
the name used is Israel, and the whole attitude
and action of the man was that of faith. In
the presentation of the boys Joseph was careful to take Manasseh, the elder, by the left
hand, so that the right hand of Jacob should
rest upon him in blessing. Israel immediately
crossed his hands, thus laying the right hand
upon the head of Ephraim, and the left upon
that of Manasseh. He then uttered the actual
words of the blessing, in which one hears
nothing save the language of triumphant confi-

dence, " The God which hath fed me all my
life long unto this day, the Angel which hath
redeemed me from all evil, bless the lads; and
let my name be named on them, and the name
of my fathers Abraham and Isaac; and let
them grow into a multitude in the midst of
the earth." There was a fine note of discrimination running through the words of this
blessing. He did not himself claim to have
walked before God. His fathers Abraham and
Isaac had done that. He did claim that He
had always fed him, and that he had been redeemed from all evil. When he said, " let my
name be named on them," he was undoubtedly
referring to the name Israel.

Joseph protested against the crossing of his
father's hands, and attempted to move the
right hand of the old man from the head of
Ephraim to that of Manasseh, because Manasseh was the firstborn.

It is evident that Israel had acted entirely
under a Divine impulse in the crossing of his
hands; and that the right hand lying on
Ephraim's head and the left upon Manasseh's
was the carrying out of a Divine purpose. It
was a moment of high inspiration, in which
Israel foresaw in clear outline the things
which were to come. In the crossing of those
hands, and the transference of the principal

blessing from the elder to the younger, he was acting as the visible agent of the God of election. Yet let it be immediately noted, and that carefully, that in the light of subsequent history it is proven that this election of God was not capricious, but in harmony with the character of the two men.

The last words of Israel to Joseph were first those in which he declared that God would be with him, and would bring him again into the land of his fathers; and secondly those in which he told him that he had given him a portion above his brethren in material possession in that land.

Notwithstanding all his faults and failures, this son of Isaac and Abraham was indeed a child of faith, and an instrument through whom it was possible for God to carry forward His purposes.

2. *Jacob's Prophecy concerning his Sons*

The last action of Jacob before his departure was that of gathering his sons about him, and foretelling their future. It is full of interest as it reveals a connection between action and issue. Jacob's forecast of the future was largely on the ground of what he had already seen in these men. In some cases the allusions are difficult to follow, and consequently the connection is not easy to discover. In other cases both are unmistakable.

In speaking of Reuben he declared that pre-eminence of privilege does not necessarily issue in pre-eminence of position. Passion uncurbed by principle, runs riot in the life; and the destined throne is never reached, nor the sceptre grasped.

Of Simeon and Levi he declared that cruelty of character ever issues in division and scattering. His statement was evidently in memory of their action in the case of the men of Shechem; and the correctness of the forecast is demonstrated by all that followed; and thus the vital importance of the great principles is made clear. Passion for right can never express itself in actions of cruelty, without evil resulting. The most distinguished son of the house of Levi in subsequent history was

Moses himself, and he was shut out from the land of possession, because out of conviction of right and consecration thereto, he yet manifested "a provoked spirit, and spake unadvisedly with his lips."

Looking at Judah, his father saw the shining of the central hope of all Israel; and he described him as of the lion nature, the perpetual type of kingship. In the distance he saw the glory of Another, Whose name Shiloh signifies peace; and it was toward that ultimate Prince of Peace that he looked with longing desire, rejoicing in Judah, because through him Shiloh would come.

His words concerning Zebulun were brief, indicating the commercial supremacy which would characterize his future.

In Issachar he saw the diplomatist, who, inspired by indolence and love of rest, would bend to service in order to secure quietness.

In Dan, the cunning and the mean, he saw the line of judgeship, and also the manifestations of treachery.

Suddenly in the midst of these forecasts a great sigh seems to have escaped from the old man, "I have waited for Thy salvation, O Jehovah." For the presence of these words here it is not easy to account. It may be that after the vision of Shiloh he had looked again at the weakness of his sons; and, therefore, his soul poured itself out in a great cry for the coming of the true Deliverer.

Resuming, he spoke of Gad as one who would be oppressed, and who yet would eventually be victorious.

For Asher he predicted prosperity, and ample supply.

In Naphtali he saw a lover of freedom, from whom godly words would flow.

When speaking of Joseph, the son of his love, he employed the most tender and beautiful language. First describing him in his fruitfulness, as " a fruitful bough "; and then revealing the secret of that fruitfulness, he was " a fruitful bough by a fountain "; he finally described the expression of the fruitfulness in declaring that " his branches run over the wall." It is indeed a perfect picture of a fruitful life. Fruitful in nature, taking hold upon the well-springs of fruitfulness, it exceeded all the bounds of expectation in its realization.

Yet Joseph had been the object of persecution, and had passed through suffering. Through all, his strength had been maintained by the Mighty One of Jacob; and abounding blessings were finally pronounced upon the head of the man who was separate from his brethren.

The word concerning Benjamin is perhaps the most perplexing; brief as it is, and revealing him as characterized by fierceness and victory.

3. *The Passing and Burial of Jacob*

Again Israel strictly charged his sons that they were to bury him with his fathers in the cave in the field of Machpelah, with Abraham and Sarah, with Isaac and Rebekah, and Leah. This is in itself significant of his faith in God, and his passion for identification with the purposes of God. Had he followed merely the dictates of human affection, he would certainly have chosen to be buried with Rachel; but in this last outlook he accounted association with Abraham and Isaac in the sleep of death of more value. Thus in faith Jacob passed unto his people.

Joseph was filled with grief, and fell upon the face of his father with weeping, and with embraces.

Then follows the account of a strange and wonderful sight, that of the burial of Jacob with Egyptian pomp in the land of promise. Evidently all the externalities were Egyptian, for the Canaanites watching said, " This is grievous mourning to the Egyptians." Yet so completely was it Hebrew that his own sons carried him into the land of promise, and buried him in Machpelah by the side of the dust of the great father and founder of the nation, Abraham.

Thus at last, after a career checkered from the beginning, Jacob entered into rest. The study of his life reveals little to his own credit, but much to the glory of the grace of God. And yet there was never wanting in his history evidence of the presence of that principle of faith, which is the basis of Divine operation. The story shines from beginning to end with the light of solemn warning, and of tender encouragement. Well will it be for us if we may avoid his mistakes; and yet amid all our failure and shortcoming it is good to remember that He Who is with us, is not alone the Lord of hosts, but also the God of Jacob.

After the sepulture, Joseph and his brethren returned to Egypt; they, filled with fear lest now that their father had departed, he should visit upon them the sin of long ago. How little they knew of the heart of their brother! Again with splendid magnanimity he triumphed over their fear, and over his own consciousness of the evil they had wrought him, by new affirmation of the fact that God was the supreme Governor. He said to them, " Ye meant evil against me, but God meant it for good."

It is always the prerogative of the man whose life is lived in close relationship to the throne of God, to be magnanimous towards those who, while attempting to harm him, do nevertheless carry out the Divine intention of blessing.

IV. OF A NATION

This final paragraph is of the nature of a page of prophetic history. We have observed the regenerative movement in the individual, in the family, and in society. In order to the accomplishment of the Divine purpose there must be a nation among the nations of the world, the depository of blessing for the sake of all the nations. Genesis does not give us the picture of that nation, but the movement towards it is seen in this final paragraph.

We have first an account of the growth and prosperity of the people. Joseph dwelt in Egypt long enough after the death of his father to see the children of Ephraim to the third generation.

Then, conscious of the approach of the hour of his own passing, he declared to his brethren that God would surely visit them, and bring them back again into the land which He sware to Abraham, to Isaac, and to Jacob; and he charged them that when they should return to that land, they were to carry up his bones with them. By that charge he also identified himself with the faith of his fathers, and declined ultimate association with Egypt.

At the age of one hundred and ten years he

passed into rest, and they embalmed him, and put him in a coffin in Egypt.

Thus ends the book of Genesis, and it is evident that it is indeed a book of beginnings, and not of consummations. To leave everything at this point is to end what commenced with the majestic declaration, " In the beginning God," and the account of the creative movement of God, in " a coffin in Egypt." Genesis demands a way out of Egypt for that coffin, or else the faith of the man whose bones rest therein, was of none effect. The name of the next book is in itself the answer to that demand—Exodus. The going out is to follow, and the coffin to find rest in the land of promise. Regeneration is not complete, but its gracious operation moved forward, and all that men of faith by faith have seen, must finally be accomplished.